THE FATHER PRINCIPLE

...RESOLVING THE INFLUENCE - RESTORING YOUR TRUTH

by

GINGER GRANCAGNOLO Ed. D.

AuthorHouse™
1663 Liberty Drive, Suite 200
Bloomington, IN 47403
www.authorhouse.com
Phone: 1-800-839-8640

AuthorHouse™ UK Ltd.
500 Avebury Boulevard
Central Milton Keynes, MK9 2BE
www.authorhouse.co.uk
Phone: 08001974150

First published by AuthorHouse 6/5/2006

ISBN: 1-4140-7462-X (e)
ISBN: 1-4184-1321-6 (sc)

Library of Congress Control Number: 2004091417

Printed in the United States of America
Bloomington, Indiana

This book is printed on acid-free paper.

Dedication

To my father, Emilio, the little giant who designed his life by hand, a unique blend of justice, fairness, unconditional service to his community, and a faith relentless with love and right action. He taught me how to go out into the world.

Table of Contents

Acknowledgments

To my great-grandfather, Salvatore, for being a true patriarch when we need it and giving us a rich heritage ... to Papa Migo for his vision and courage to trust change as he directed his family to honor Italian culture while staying anchored in American patriotism no matter what ... to Papa Larry, the most consistently gentle, simple man I've ever known ... to Jose Silva, founder of Silva International, whose dedication to his dream produced tangible, scientific proof of the Power within us through his original genius program, "The Silva Method" ... to Fr. Albert Gorayeb, my forever priest, teacher, friend—his memory remains with me always.

Introduction

Have you ever noticed a certain something inside as you've casually said, "This is my father," "Wait 'til you meet my father," "Not my Dad," "He/she reminds me of my father"?

If you were to freeze frame those common moments, maybe you would hear your inner dialogue and notice a flash of feelings that you thought you didn't have or that you finally remembered.

These moments can be so subtle, quiet, and brief, yet their effects can profoundly linger. These moments can transport you back in time as if you stepped into your childhood while looking at a family photo. Sometimes this time shift can be an oasis for the heart and a clearing for the mind. And of course, an ordinary Dad flashback can rip through your soul like an unsuspecting attacker's knife.

The point to be made here is not whether your father tales are pleasant or painful but rather that they remained, influenced, and shaped you. An even deeper point is that there is a Father Principle in everyone that is as certain as the energy of Dad's DNA, and that it was meant to teach you, stir you, and empower you regardless of the quality of the relationship you and your father had—if you know how to feel it, use it, and know its real truth.

These pages are about releasing the hidden jewels your father relationship meant for you, to inherit, and to give you a new choice about whom you can be. Having been enriched by an innovative understanding about Dad's genes, habits, and your relationship with him, you can become "father to your-self," able to re-create you "into the highest version of your highest vision" everyday through everyday circumstances.[1]

The interesting phenomenon about this seemingly impossible miracle is that your biological father and/or father-figures do not have to be aware of their influence in order for you to tap into the buried treasure all dads inherently give us. The reason for this is the core of this work. It is called the Father Principle. The Father Principle is an energetic blueprint, embedded in the inner consciousness in everyone. It is a major archetype. An archetype is like a code or a bionic "chip" that holds pure facts. The Father Principle "chip" carries every detail pertinent to the father universal law of energy. This law gives guidelines about the power to go out into the world successfully, to be somebody and do something that may leave a signature of goodness in your name. All of us are already "coded" to potentially know this. The relationship with biological fathers and father-figures "triggers"

---

[1] Neale Donald Walsch, Conversation With God, Book I (New York: G.P. Putnam's Sons, 1995), 20.

this potential and for better or worse, Dads strike the chip. What happens after that is up to each individual choice.

My own Dads' chip was sparked by many uniquely different experiences. I am of Italian American roots, privileged to grow up in a multigenerational household. My great-grandfather, Salvatore, born in Naples, Italy, fathered sixteen children, went to church every day, designed the original gas lines in Newark, New Jersey, had beautiful blue eyes, thick, white, wavy hair, a keen wit with everyone. Grandpa drank wine and smoked a "stogie" daily (a small, thin, tightly wrapped cigar, whose aroma could take the glue off of twenty-year-old wallpaper). His stature was short, yet obliviously regal. He was the tribal patriarch—proud, willful, always convincing. He outlived my great-grandmother by twenty years. He gave me a sense of heritage, revealing a look at family tribal dynamics, a real feel for "genetic history," and the potential promise of a long life. Grandpa died at 100 of natural causes.

My maternal grandfather, Papa Larry, was orphaned by three years old and raised by his siblings. He was gentle, kind, soft-spoken, an outstanding cook of Napoletano palate pleasers, and lovingly nurtured Nana's every need. He showed me the kindness of a provider. I loved working in the vegetable garden with Papa. He taught me how to watch the wind to know when it was going to rain and how to rotate the vegetables so not to wear out the soil. To please me, Papa Larry planted watermelons—my favorite! That year, the crop didn't seem to take for some reason. I was about seven years old at the time and to keep the wonderment alive Papa carefully placed huge, store-bought watermelons close to the vines. The next morning we went routinely to water our precious crops and, lo and behold, I thought we had been visited by the powerful watermelon fairy! Of course, we shared the surprise joke with lots of laughter. I am so grateful to have been impressed by his demonstration of the softer side of men.

Papa Migo, Dominick, was my paternal grandfather. A native of Catania, Sicily, he carried over a long line of cultural customs and values. He was the clear Italian-American icon, a blend of old-world, strict, unnegotiable family traditions and of new-world dreams, anchored in patriotism and the right to vote. So every Sunday was clearly defined. First we went to church, followed by endless midday "antipasto"—cheese, bread, Marsala wine, roasted peppers, and demitasse coffee. These were served for hours, serenaded by opera on the radio and the sounds of the side door repeatedly opening and closing, making way for uncles, aunts, and scores of cousins who somehow looked alike! We lived "upstairs" from Papa Migo. What a treat! Our days and nights were filled with routines, kissing everyone in the house, upstairs and downstairs, no matter how many times anyone would come in and out. But for me, the after-dinner ritual left me permanently jeweled. Papa would have me sit on his lap while he was romancing his espresso slowly. When he would get to the last ounce, he would put in an extra bit of sugar and feed it to me, and in a low, smiling voice, he'd say, "Buono, e?" There were other faces of Papa Migo as well. He was rivetingly strict. Sometimes it would jolt me stiff. He was progressive. We had the first color TV on the block. He was without hesitation the first and last word in the family. He was an honest, good businessman, and because of this proud posture I never saw him in anything but a white, starched shirt. Because of him, my earliest days on North Twelfth Street in Newark, New Jersey, were the safest memories I own.

The deepest, richest father imprints I wear are from my own father, Emilio. He was a lot like his father, only better. My father is the single, most-honest man of integrity I've ever known. He is a little man, with a giant love for God, devotion to my mother, and a sacrificing perseverance for both me and my brother. I have never known my father to make a wrong decision when it came to his family. This should not imply that I liked everything about him growing up. Dad was unshakable when he said "no" or "yes" to our requests. This is not always a teenage girl's favorite ally! My father was a design engineer with an incredibly precise, exacting mind for details and "best outcomes"—again, not my favorite when I wanted to do things "my way." He was always affectionate, while remaining absolutely clear about what was supposed to be done now in the house, for school, etc. All it would take was one of his eyebrows to arch up, and I knew it meant trouble! No matter what, I always knew my father loved me. He once told me, as I was pushing for my way, that it wasn't his job to have me like him, but that it was his job, given to him by God, to keep me safe, guided, and protected. Now, how was I supposed to argue with that?

These images release a kaleidoscope of feelings in me, bringing both laughter and tears. Not all memories and their effects were pleasant. But the single, most-significant seed my father cultivated in me is that he always told the truth, no matter what. It is his fortitude for endurance, a shield for life's stress. It became mine, as well. This seed will continue to feed me for all the seasons of my life!

Good or bad memories, forgotten or blocked, I invite you to journey through these pages—to perhaps laugh or cry, but mostly to rebuild and get into the world more powerfully certain of your-Self than ever before!

If you choose to, let us begin—

Our Father, Who art in Heaven,

Hallowed be Thy name.

Thy Kingdom come, Thy will be done,

On earth as it is in Heaven.

Give us this day our daily bread,

And forgive us our trespasses as

We forgive those who trespass against us,

And lead us not into temptation,

But deliver us from evil

Now and forever and ever. Amen.

Chapter One : Who Is Your Father?

Who is this man? What is he really like? Did you get to know him, his feelings, dreams, strengths, weaknesses? What did he do with his broken dreams, or his wounded heart? Was he even there—physically, emotionally? Was he fair? Did you feel his love?

If you were to really ponder these questions, I'm sure your reactions would stir both positives and negatives. And if you were to allow for your own deep introspection, you would probably see some similar characteristic of Dad laced into your personality fabric as well. Then maybe you might say, "Well, what should I expect? That's where I came from!"

1

If you were to see yourself merely from this psychobiological casting, you would be correct. However, the premise here is deeper. It is deeper than chromosomes and attitudes. It is about the power of archetypes implanted in the inner conscious energy of the Life Force we constantly breathe

The archetype, as Jung conceived it, is a precondition and coexistent of life itself; its manifestations not only reach upwards to the spiritual heights of religion, art, and metaphysics, but also down into the dark realms of organic and inorganic matter. Both Jung and ethology appear to provide some satisfaction for a fundamental human need—the need to perceive meaning, the need to comprehend.[2]

A major archetype, then, is the father archetype. Its principles can define how you relate to the world, how you perceive that the world identifies you.

It was in his 1909 paper that Jung first stated his opinion that the seemingly 'magical' hold and influence that parents have over their children was not merely a function of their individual personalities, or of the child's relative helplessness, but was primarily due to the numinosity of the parental archetypes activated by them in the child's psyche. The personal father inevitably embodies the archetype, which is what endows this figure with its fascinating power. The archetype acts as an amplifier, enhancing beyond measure the effects that proceed from the father, so far as these conform to the inherited pattern.[3]

---

[2] Dr. Anthony Stevens, Archetypes (London, England: Routledge & Kegan Ltd., 1982), 29.
[3] Stevens, Archetypes, p. 104.

The inner patterns released beyond biology and circumstance shall be called the "Father Principle." In myths, legends, dreams the Father Principle is meant to personify the Elder, the King, the Father in Heaven. It is the lawgiver of collective authority and the living embodiment of the Logos, a Greek word meaning his word is law. In other, more poetic interpretations, Logos suggests the Divine Ordering factor of the Universe.

From this root meaning, several keywords illustrate the far-reaching dynamics of the Father Principle as it is observed in your everyday experiences. The Father Principle in its male energy in all of us is assertiveness, responsibility, reputation, provider, creator-builder, government, military, clergy, CEO, guardian of status quo, bastion against all enemies, the high noon sun, phallus, weapons, patriarch, chronological time. General of cause and effect, reward and punishment, he allows you to find law, orderliness, and to project, to do, out in the world.

The Father Principle is concerned with events of the tangible world. It is focused on events that are approached, controlled, and modified through knowingness and an act of will. It is not only about the father's attitudes towards work, social achievement, politics, and the discipline to develop his children that forms you. But more precisely that the Father Principle, as demonstrated through your father and father-figures, ought to have succeeded in freeing you from the security involvement with your mother in order to obtain the necessary autonomy for effective living.[4]

---

[4] Stevens, Archetypes, p. 108.

I am clear that most Dads may or may not sufficiently create this awareness and suitable skills for life. Fear not! The magic still awaits you! It is energetically embossed upon your soul through the power of the archetype.

The key, then, is to know how to get the magical script out of the inner consciousness, to heal neglects and go forward! To satisfy this need to connect and correct the inside potential to the outer world actualization, it would be helpful, easy, and effective to use the "Prayer Room" exercises at the end of each chapter. Each exercise is to serve you as a specific technique to resolve unaware father influences, to change the blind and chronic effects and to choose a new, more-appropriate determination for your personal and professional success.

The simplest way to create your "Prayer Room" is to just go through the following experience.

Prayer Room Exercise

- Be comfortable, in a sitting position.
- Adjust your body so you can remain quiet for a few moments.
- Close your eyes and take three deep, slow breaths.
- With eyes closed for the rest of this exercise, imagine you are at the top of a staircase with ten golden, lighted, descending steps.
- Continue to visualize descending each step, slowly, even feeling the Golden Light ascending up your legs, through the soles of your feet.
- Take your time, and continue to breathe deeply and slowly as you count

from one to ten silently to yourself.

- At the count of ten, you will be at the base of the staircase, standing in a silver-lighted doorway.

- Now, at the count of three, you will pass through the silver-lighted doorway, saying silently to yourself, "I seek peace."

- One, two three. Now you are in a room that shall be called your "Prayer Room."

- Be very creative—decide all dimensions, floor, ceiling, walls, colors.

- Create a skylight in the center of the ceiling to allow an imaginary beam of blue-white light to connect you to the center of the universe.

- You may say silently here, "As above, so below."

- Create a comfortable chair, lounge, etc., that you will sit in every time you are in your "Prayer Room."

- Create the proper lighting that pleases you.

- Create where this "Prayer Room" is; imagine it to be in a private wooded area, near a lake, or a get-away beach house on a remote tropical island.

- Be freely creative! This is your personal, private "Prayer Room."

- Create flowers, fountains, open, spacious windows with a beautiful view.

- Be certain to remember that the center beam of blue-white light is the life force that is always connected to you. It is the very Power and Presence of God.

- Now be relaxed, sitting in your chair, and allow the blue-white light to shine all over you, even through you.

- Repeat several times, silently, "Peace, peace, peace."

- Now just listen and trust your first impressions; just let the experience be, without judgment.

- Feel, sense, your personal responses ...

  - Do you believe that there is the Power Source of All Life, always breathing within you?

  - Can you feel, sense the Power, know that Power, and let it just relax you?

  - Do you know that your breathing, every breath, is the Breath of God? You are always breathing the Divine Source of Peace, Joy, Healing, no matter what, simply because you're breathing, by day and by night, unaware or aware the Power breathes in you, always, now and always.

- Continue to relax, breathing the blue-white light in an easy, steady manner, in and out, in and out, occasionally repeating to yourself, "Peace, peace, peace."

- Whenever you are ready to complete these prayerful moments, just say "thank you" and walk back through the silver-lighted doorway, then ascend back up the ten steps of Golden Light, and back out to outer awareness.

- Then open your eyes, more relaxed and at peace with yourself.

This Prayer Room exercise will be used at the end of every chapter with a particular healing function in mind.

Chapter Two : The Child is Father of the Man

As you look into a mirror, can you say with any amount of certainty, "How much is me? How much is just sticky residue?" The accurate response is a tightly woven cross stitch of both. You acquired an imitative pattern of parental impressions made mostly by age three or four and an ongoing design of personality intricacies created by your experiences that continue to make adjustments upon the original foundational threads.

It appears that much of who you think you are is established by about three years old and as you become language literate. When you began to speak in some formation of sentences, you began to notice the power of relationship as you connected through these early stages of cause and effect. You learned yourself as you used even the simplest expressions of yes and no.

What you were not aware of, however, is the fact that your brain had already recorded the deeper influence, which for this discussion I will call "Father I-dents." Using the metaphor "eye-dents" can make this understanding certainly more impactful.

If you imagine your eyes to be like a camcorder since you were an infant, with the "record" button constantly on, you'd truly see that your brain has stored all the stories, voice tones, unusual and usual postures, facial expressions, emotions, and personality nuances of Dad as you were growing up, mostly without your conscious awareness.

The brain does function like a camcorder, accurately keeping thousands of detailed message units in the inner conscious mind. Within you is a well-organized library of memories, thoughts, feelings, experiences both positive and negative, all neatly arranged and "safe" at a specific dimension of the mind called the alpha brain wave frequency.[5] The alpha brain wave frequency is a specific frequency scientifically determined to be in the range of seven to fourteen cycles per second. This frequency occurs several times during the night as you sleep. It is the frequency that occurs when dreaming, regardless of whether it is a nighttime or daytime dream. The alpha frequency

---

[5] Jose Silva, The Silva Mind Control Method (New York: Simon & Schuster, Inc., 1977), 19-20.

is commonly known as the Relaxation response, a noticeable, measurable brainwave frequency at a meditative state, witnessed as R.E.M.—rapid eye movement. This frequency is the record-button.[6] Whatever is experienced while at the alpha brain frequency is imprinted upon the brain and will automatically determine a behavior based on that imprint, regardless of it being consciously or unconsciously perceived. What is more important is that the brain remains at the alpha cycle about 75 percent of the time up until you are about seven or eight years old. This is the cause of your Dad I-dents and the subsequent behavioral effects that have manifested in your life.

It is the inside you that has created the outside you.[7] Perception made your projection onto others and your world. Because these imprints were made so long ago, you think it is you. It feels normal, habitual, and for better or worse you may have concluded, "This is just the way I am."

An extremely significant correction is necessary here. This is who you have become, but not <u>all</u> of who you really are.

To further highlight the Dad I-dents behavior formation, a favorite poem is worth mentioning:

My Heart Leaps Up

By William Wordsworth (1807)

My heart leaps up when I behold

A rainbow in the sky:

So was it when my life began;

---

[6] Wayne Dyer, Manifest Your Destiny (New York: Harper Collins, 1997), 57.
[7] Deepak Chopra, The Seven Spiritual Laws of Success (San Rafael, CA: Amber-Allen & New World Library, 1993), 39.

So is it now I am a man;

So be it when I shall grow old;

Or let me die!

The Child is father of the Man;

And I could wish my days to be

Bound each to each in natural piety.

The masterful poet has captured the mystical truth of cause and effect that pierces through time and space much like the arch of the rainbow stretching through rain clouds! What he didn't know is that technology would give back the hope to the man so that the child-like creativity from within would always be available to rebirth the self even better than before.[8] Through decades of research, Jose Silva and his genius program, "The Silva Method," demonstrated that by using a particular technique you can go into that library of the mind and change any undesirable effects as well as create new causes for new goals and success patterns.

The Prayer Room exercises to be used at the end of every chapter are based on this wonderful data! To connect from within alpha, then, is to correct the actions and blind behaviors that have limited your full capacity to be fully you.

The releasing combination to heal you is to imagine the Father Principle universal codes and your Dad I-dents like two transparencies stuck together and stored at the alpha dimensions. What is etched within is the pure imprint

---

[8] James Allen, As a Man Thinketh (New York: Barnes & Noble, 1992), 19.

of a Universal Father in all His Power ready to be used by you every time you are in the Prayer Room and the recorded imprints of your father and father figures stuff. The Father Principle Chip is as timeless as your soul. The Dad I-dents are temporal and changeable.

If you could play back your camcorder tape on a full screen movie of "This Is Your Life," you'd see the indelible images of the Father Principle, i.e., good use of authority, the Creator, a loving, protective Father, leader of truth, order and justice, a visionary for humanity, independent, skillful, willful towards the good of all. Then you would see an overlayer of images, faces of your Dad, uncles, grandfathers, teachers, coaches that would appear like a decoupage of both your positive and negative experiences. Your behaviors, actions, expressions are rooted and triggered by this ongoing movie in its double-exposure version. The end result is that sometimes you're you echoing out all that is anchored in the empowered Father Principle you, and sometimes the undesirable Dad I-dents are running you. Your robot-like actions seem at this point to be out of your control. They are not—just merely out of your reach if you are not aware of the healing properties of your Prayer Room.

The more you quietly spend time in your Prayer Room, the more awareness is gifted to you. Your internal library becomes more inviting. You are able to read you with more light on the pages of your life and with more incentive to rewrite chapters both now and then with more hope, determination, and conviction that you can change the emotional effects if they no longer define who you really want to be. It is important to note that the first step in this healing process is to be aware of the Dad imprints and to decide what you want to change, what you are willing to change. Then new patterns and impressions can be made with greater effectiveness. Like the phrase, "It is not wise to put clean water in a dirty vessel," the washing away can begin through this following exercise.

Prayer Room Exercise:
"Identifying Your Father Imprints"

- Use the same procedure to enter into your Prayer Room as outlined in Chapter One.
- Take your time, repeatedly breathing in and out in an easy, rhythmic manner.
- Be more aware, creative with the design of your Prayer Room.
- Add any details you desire, color, texture; use all your senses to enhance the experience— sight, hearing, taste, smell, touch.
- Allow yourself to be sitting in your chair or lounge now and sense the Blue White Light from above pouring all around you, even through you.
- Now relax and listen inside yourself to the responses to these questions.
- Be honest, spontaneous, without judging the experience.
- Imagine, sense your father to be right in front of you, feel his presence, just observe him, take your time.
- What is the first feeling you feel? Is it positive? Negative?
- Is this a usual, common feeling you have for him?

- Continue, as much as possible, to stay focused on your feelings.
- Now allow your mind to have several random flashbacks, five years ago, ten, twenty, as far back into early childhood as possible.
- Take your time and pause as long as you like for any one memory; allow for any and <u>all</u> emotions.
- As you are re-viewing these Dad scenes, repeat often to yourself, "Peace, Peace, Peace."
- Now, just trust your first impressions.
    - How are you most like your father?
    - Do you respond to life, people with the same or similar emotional ways?
    - Do you still re-play your father imprints with regard to commitments, honor, control, authority, faith, God, keeping your word?
    - Are you still feeling controlled, limited by his values, wishes, expectations of you?
    - Do you respect him? Government? Those in charge?
    - Can you self-motivate at any time?
    - Do you feel your career path is really fulfilling your life's purpose?
    - Do you persevere in times of struggle, crisis?
    - Are you angry with him or anyone else and can't seem to completely get rid of it?
    - Do you have to win?
    - Do you blame outside forces for your limitations of happiness, i.e, salary, education, government, employer, church?
    - Do you really feel in-charge of yourself, your life's joy?

13

- Take your time feeling and silently responding to each question.

- After completing all questions as clearly as you can, then repeat several times, "I am determined to see me differently."

- When you are peaceful and ready to do so, simply conclude the exercise by saying "Thank you" and ascend the ten steps of Golden Light, back out to outer conscious awareness.

It is advised to complete this exercise several times. Your awareness increases every time. It is also good to write feelings and/or responses in a journal for further reflection.

Chapter Three : Responsibility and Reputation vs. Obligation and Burden

A paramount projection stemming from distorted Father I-dents and an imbalanced display of the Father Principle is the weakened quality of the work world caused by conflicting values towards responsibility and reputation. However, if the Father Principle had a clear path for expression, it would best be seen as prideful effort and personal integrity in all that had to do with the work force or your career. It would get you out into the world, motivated by sharing individualized talents that would serve the whole and build a community. The Father Principle fuels you to stand up in the world and to be responsible no matter what, to truth, quality, and honor towards fellow humankind.

You may know this as your ideal career mission statement, yet conversely realize you and work colleagues may not see eye to eye. So often the workplace is a checkerboard of those who want to excel from some inner purpose vs. those who are driven by personal profits and a vision of a secure and earlier retirement. Others you know may have insulated themselves into their "own little world," not willing to stretch a single inch past what was defined in their original job descriptions. Disheartened by the have and have-nots in life, they remain corralled by their self-victimizing attitudes and behaviors. They stay in their anger and blame, ready to deliver their self-justification speeches at any family gathering. You may watch these isolates go to work frustrated and come home depleted. Day after day, routine runs them lifeless.

This powerless scenario illustrates the blocked Father Principle guarded from its true definition of responsibility. The archetype within knows that responsibility really means able to respond, with a choice—positive or negative. This innate ability of choice—reaction—cleanses your perception so that you stop viewing life's everyday circumstances as a personal attack, leaning in on you because you're slated to remain one of the lowly ones! Staying unconnected to the true power of the Father Principle, I believe, has created an epidemic of adult immaturity in our society over the last several decades. This dis-eased emotional condition can be observed every day, everywhere. On your way to work, you may witness a daily dose of road rage, numb and uninvolved human beings, egotistical competition, cutting corners, littering, fatty product control, misuse of monies, tax laws, stock tips, and company perks, to name a few. What seems more infectiously damaging is that for most this appears normal, acceptable. All of this, you may have heard, is seemingly "the way of the world."

From this foiled Father Principle power, reputation may no longer be an earned honor, but rather a well-marketed image. The result is your ability to maintain personal truth becomes demoralized. It becomes a burden, a heavy-hearted responsibility to stay real and unaffected by those smiling through the illusory world of success that some have created. You may have even said, "It doesn't pay to be a good guy!"

If you have struggled with this journey for truth, rejoice, pilgrim! Your wandering travels are over! Remembering the power imprint of able to respond and staying connected to the Light within the Prayer Room on a regular basis keeps you grounded, more relaxed, clear-minded, and in charge of your emotional life. You may not always be the authority of daily situations. You can be in the director's chair of how you let it affect you. This can be a real awakening to everyday joy simply because you've chosen to stay self-responsive. A most-potent trigger to staying connected to the Light of the Father Principle is to keep your word! This sounds easy to acknowledge and is more difficult to practice[9]—to keep your word literally mean everything, always. Precisely put, say what you mean and mean what you say, to everyone, firstly yourself. Not keeping your word to yourself automatically severs your anchor to the Within. You become a house divided. From this separation you become vulnerable to your own guilt,

[9] Don Miguel Ruiz, The Four Agreements (San Rafael, CA: Amber-Allen, 1997), 25.

shame, lack of confidence, and self-worth. You can easily then try to set up a shield of protection so that others don't sense your self-imposed failure. You then further create the self-defensive blame game, out-of-control, tailspinning, Victim Drama Saga, that most of your listeners may not even comprehend. You can then silently, consciously or unconsciously, think yourself irresponsible. From this, you re-create yourself less powerful than necessary. The power of your own words is truly magical.

I learned this from my father. He ALWAYS kept his word. ALWAYS. Good or bad, his promises were REAL. If a reward were in order, I could count on it. The opposite was also equally true. From early on, I could see the Power of the Word, the cause and effect of it. I could feel a sense of order and safety in this. Boundaries were clear. When I was a young child, boundaries were not negotiable. As I grew, this keep-your-word policy translated into my own personality dynamics, as an ability to be organized and self-motivated. If I said it, I did it!

Self-reliance,[10] even though a natural process for the mind brain-body phenomenon, seems to have to be taught, and often with great resistance. Self-reliance is personal freedom. It enables you to live your life without the emotional entanglements of others' opinions and judgments. Self-reliance, self-responsibility is not a borderline compulsion. In fact, a major flag of distorted Father Principle empowerment is chronic procrastination and its opposite compulsiveness to a driven end. You may identify some as work

[10] Henri J. Nourven, Here and Now (New York: Crossroads Publishing, 1994), 113.

warriors armed by a constant display of cell phone in one hand, beeper in the other, fueled by caffeine and power bars, always pushing to "stay on top," to get the successful deal now. There seems to be no real peace in this, no balance of family, silence, and simple pleasures. Sometimes these work warriors will say they are doing it for their families, so that they can have more. Having more is not being more. Being more is the act of self-re-creation sourced by an endless Universal Father Creator Light that has been given to all His children equally. Using it is up to you and it is priceless.

This responsibility imbalance is also demonstrated by those who just do too much. They have over-packed schedules, projects at home, carting children in vans back and forth to every school and social event, finally to collapse into bed without taking a moment all day to quietly look into the eyes of a loved one, to smile, find or give comfort, or to say, "I love you, today."

Responsibility to life doesn't always mean to constantly push your wheelbarrow up a greased hill. It means to decide your dreams, goals, values, and then become co-creator, using your God-Creator-Builder Light from within. It makes the journey of life so much more enjoyable. Shut the TV, computers, phones, video games OFF! Make time for SILENCE and find what really makes YOU happy, what makes you feel your BEST!!

I am reminded here of a favorite children's song:

Row, row, row your boat,

Gently down the stream.

Merrily, merrily, merrily, merrily,

Life is but a dream.

Notice it says, "row YOUR boat"! Perhaps your first step towards personal happiness is to keep your oars in your own boat! Then it says "gently down the stream." Are you gentle in your attitude towards yourself and others? And did you know that attitude is a chosen response to life that you can make at any moment? Happiness is not a dream, or an afterglow of having accomplished a particular goal. It is a choice you make in yourself, for yourself, because then you can respond to life more powerfully if you do.

Choose, with all you really are now, to relax and complete the next Prayer Room exercise.

Prayer Room Exercise: "How Responsible Are You?"

- Enter into your Prayer Room as suggested in Chapter One.
- Once in the Prayer Room, relax in your chair, lounge and take several deep breaths, slowly, in and out.
- Sense, visualize, feel the Blue White Light from above pouring through you.
- Take your time.
- Sense the balance all around you, in all that you have created in your beautiful Prayer Room—flowers, fountains, a beautiful view.
- Just relax and sense your first true feelings.
  - Do you feel overburdened with everyday life?
  - Do you take time for yourself to just be quiet, undisturbed every

day?

- Are you trapped by others' opinions, judgments?
- Do you keep your word to yourself? To others?
- Do you laugh enough, cry enough, pray enough, play enough?
- Do you stay in charge of your reactions to life's events and choose constructive peace over conflict?
- Do you hold on to could have, should have, would have?
- Do you hold on to negative emotions about yourself, others?
- Are you influenced by media, trends, worldly standards of happiness and success, that may not be in your best regard?
- Are you living your own honest values every day?

• Continue to relax and ask the Blue White Light to cleanse you of confusion and illusions, letting only what is peaceful and in your highest good to remain.

• Take your time; when you are ready, say "Thank you."

• Count out, back up the ascending stairs of Golden Light steps.

Chapter Four : The Power of Be-Cause

Your life is the way it is, because the sum total of all your thoughts, feelings, and experiences, both consciously and subconsciously, caused it to be that way.

At first hearing this, you may react with upset, anger, sadness, or disbelief. You may say, "How could that be? Why would I create pockets of unfulfillment like money problems, chronic pain, unrequited love, and splintered dreams, fragmented in youth?"

The key to the TRUTH—What you think about, you bring about—is firstly that this is as certain as the law of gravity. This fact is a core function of the Father Principle. The Father Principle is the Logos, the ordering factor in all of the universe. It keeps the stability of the Creation Law. The pure fuel of this law is energy itself, and that energy is constantly moving towards the direction you are leading it into. Your life's circumstances are the direct effect of you being co-creator with the Creator's Essence (Pure Energy) and by the act of your thinking specific ideas, images, desires, feelings, that became the creation-manifestation you are now living. You've heard this so many times in so many ways, yet the real power of it may have escaped you. Thoughts are things.[11] My banner for this law is What I say for me is true for me.

A beautiful description of this is best painted in the Old Testament, first book of Genesis:[12] "In the beginning was the WORD and the WORD was God." If you unfold this phrase, you can see a partnership of Power. Word + God = My thoughts + God's energy = My Life's Creation. Further on in the scripture reference, you can read:[13] "God said, 'Let there be Light,' and

[11] Louise Hay, You Can Heal Your Life (Santa Monica, CA: Hay House, Inc., 1984), 43.
[12] Bible, Genesis 1:1-2.
[13] Bible, Genesis 1:3-4.

there was Light." Again, you can see the Law of Creation (Father Principle) at work. God said and it was made so.

I can read these lines over and over and always be overflowing in my heart with the realization of just how powerful humankind really is. Lack of power, then, is not the problem; lack of skillful awareness is. Mostly, you may have been attempting to create your life to match your dreams by doing something outside yourself to make it happen.

The shift here, due to the formula-law of the Father Principle, is to "Be with the Being" from within, see, feel, create your intention and then allow the Power of Being to now guide, direct, influence your doing, to effectively materialize your dreams, hopes, wishes.

Does this seem magical? It is. Look deeper into the true definition of magic. Its root is derived from the word magi, wise. Wisdom for true happiness awaits you from the Within.[14] Seek first the Kingdom of Heaven and all else shall follow. Through the research and documentation of Jose Silva, this kingdom is now measurable at 10 cycles per second of brainwave frequency, known as the alpha dimension.[15]

Years of blood, sweat, and tears proved that this inner wisdom-magic is available to everyone, is easy to achieve, and is free![16] It is the Father in Heaven's good pleasure to give you the kingdom and to give it to you abundantly.

---

[14] Bible, Proverbs 3:13-18.
[15] Robert Stone, Ph.D., The Secret Life of Your Cells (West Chester, PA: Whitford Press, 1989), 74.
[16] Don Miguel Ruiz, The Mastery of Love (San Rafael, CA: Amber-Allen Publishing, Inc., 1999), 91.

The king-dom is real and present always. Your lack of skillful awareness to this inner sanctuary and its power to create has often made your inner silence feel like a dungeon. It is time to put the lights on and release your own buried treasures!

For too long, powerful, unaware thoughts and feelings have been building your life's circumstances into a mixture, a series of mishaps, mild successes, moments of joy, and unsuspected disappointments, all victim to the unanswered question, "Why?"

The marriage of science and spirituality can help to answer this now. If you were to look at a tree full grown, as you held an acorn in your hand, you may be stunned by the illogical connection. If you were to slice a richly ripened red tomato and carefully take a tiny white seed, separate it from its domed habitat, wait for it to dry, then gently pierce it, you would not find minuscule tomatoes waiting to become plump. All you would find is the thin-air miracle. This is the Power and the Promise of the Father Creator in all of life. We are that life!

In the acorn is the promise of a thousand forests. Your thoughts create your forests, your gardens, or your cemeteries.

Be aware—to truly be at the cause of your life's path, you must be at the cause of your thoughts and then responsible for your feelings and their results. It is as certain as Law.

So much of your life has already been stored in an unaware manner in the library of your alpha mind. Tucked away by years, it may seem impossible to you to cause a change from the past, let alone create a new cause for the future. This is not so. Because thoughts and feelings are purely only energy, another aspect of Father Principle Law helps us to reclaim our inner power. Energy can neither be destroyed nor created, only transformed.[17] Translated to your everyday experiences, this means you can't change what happened, only how it influenced you, thereby giving you the charge to re-create a new tomorrow, today. The point of Power is always in the present (Presence).

With your new construct for past, present, future based in energy laws and not psychological assumptions, it must be a priority to use your Prayer Room daily. Going into your Prayer Room is creatively using the alpha dimension. By listening, trusting, creating new ideas, thoughts, goals from your Prayer Room, you can begin to create a congruent life. You allow the inside power to direct the outside world more positively than ever before. To assure and reinforce these inside gems, you must watch your words to express the same positive treasured intents. Be aware! Unless you are willing to change your words, you are NOT willing to change! Speak the words and your soul shall be healed.

Affirm your life's intentions inside yourself from the Prayer Room by filling it with peace and positive pictures. Then, bolster this by daily affirmations and clear, concise, happy self-talk. You have nothing to lose by doing this but weakness.

One of my favorite affirmations is, "I am calm and confident." I say it often, daily, nightly, and for no reason, just be-cause! I partly make this statement so frequently because of watching my father solve problems.

---

[17] Ernest Holmes, The Science of Mind (New York, NY: Dodd, Mead and Co., 1938), 68.

My father was an architectural design engineer. Specifically, he was a space efficiency expert for hotels, restaurants, schools, commercial sites. He participated in the designing of four pavilions in the 1963 World's Fair in New York. As I would watch him think, he would sit calmly, creating images in his mind for long periods of time. He would almost gaze out of focus and then, in a blink, his pencil would create the perfect form. I would go to him as a child to ask him to fix something—a loosened skate, a twisted gear on my bike, a chip broken from a favorite figurine. I would immediately present my solution as if to say, "Just do this and hurry up so I can play." He would slowly look at it, turn it in all directions, look again and again without a word. Sometimes in my girlish witnessing, I would murmur to myself, "I hope he knows what he is doing." Then, after long pauses and some kind of manipulations, Dad would release the project back to me and say, "Here, honey, it's okay now." I'd look, review it, and again murmur from inside, "How did he do that?" It was calmly, confidently done.

Another reason I enjoy this power phrase is because it appears to be an antidote to our cultural style. For some, calm may mean just before Rest in Peace and confident, unfortunately, may mean push with arrogance. Dad showed me neither were true.

The best affirmations are those following "I am." Make your own. Make them short, to the point. Feel them. Live them.

Anchor them from your Prayer Room to allow them to become your natural expressions for living. Let us use an exercise to clear some past negativities and to put you back into the power present more ready to direct your future.

Prayer Room Exercise: "Are You Ready to Influence Your Own Life?"

- Use the entrance ritual into your Prayer Room as outlined in Chapter One.

- Once inside your Prayer room, take your time and take several deeper breaths, slowly, silently repeating, "Peace, Peace, Peace."

- Now just continue in a relaxed manner to respond honestly, openly to the following questions:

  - Do you really feel, believe you are influencing, causing your own happiness? Success? Well-being?

  - Where do you feel or believe you're being influenced at work, home, family, friends, self-image?

  - Who or what seems to be influencing, steering, directing you?

  - What happens to your emotions when you don't feel constructively in charge of yourself?

  - Do you push back (hiding inside or leaning with pressure on others) when you don't feel or believe you are free to express?

  - Are these results positive/negative and do you honestly claim responsibility for your own results?

  - Are your inside thoughts or feelings equal to your outside expressions? Why or why not?

  - Are you ready NOW to be at the cause of your whole life, spiritually, mentally, financially, emotionally, physically? Why or why not?

  - Do you understand that unless you are willing to be at the cause of your life, you can't exercise the real power inside to affect or influence a real change in your life?

– Where and/or why do you still feel like a victim of circumstances?

– Are you willing to do what it takes to change these situations now, from inside you first, then with more positive attitudes and actions?

– What is really keeping you from using your inside power, right NOW, daily, forever?

– What do you think you are gaining by remaining a victim in certain situations?

– Are you really ready to be the Prime Influence of your life and well-being? If so, begin to use the following affirmations daily—

- I am calm and confident.

- I see the TRUTH in all situations.

- I stay anchored to my Creator Father Power through daily silence in my Prayer Room.

- I am as happy as I make up my mind and heart to be.

- I am choosing clear, positive thoughts, attitudes, feelings, and actions, always.

- I am the cause of my greatness.

- I am guided, directed to good, divine, right actions, as I am always rooted in the Pure Power of Father Creator Goodness and Abundance.

- I am the Peace, Joy of my Father Creator Power now and always.

• Take your time with each affirmation, really feeling the Blue White

Light entering in you and surrounding you.

- Focus in an easy peace with each affirmation so that you can really become it.

- When you are finished, breathe again, say, "Peace, Peace, Peace"—and then say, "Thank you."

- Count out ten to one, ascending the Golden Light steps, back out to outer consciousness.

It is also recommended that you write these affirmations and verbally repeat them daily to reinforce more immediate and long-lasting effects.

Chapter Five : Now and Then—Changing the Effects in Relationships

No one's father was perfect. He wasn't supposed to be. No matter who your father was or wasn't, his job was not to be a pristine reflection of the perfect Father Principle archetype. He was only to be a lamp to get you to find that securely hidden soul imprint. Perfection is God's signature. You were designed to be triggered by Dad and/or father figure types so that you would be motivated to search for that inherited Divine perfection. Dad's personality and character traits were imperfectly perfect to jump start your process to self-creation. Erroneously you might have relied on Dad or father figures to be your answers to getting out in the world, establishing a marker for success and choosing good, loving relationships. They were only meant to rub you the right way or the wrong way, so that you would ultimately seek the truth from within and thereby be sourced by the Divine Father, forever.

Everyone has father wounds. They begin early, blindly, and can remain that way forever. These cuts can make openings, pathways to the Divine if you follow the beam of light deeper and deeper into the true Self. It can be a long process because so many Dad I-dents occur without you realizing it.

Have you ever watched a Dad and a little son walk side by side, and they rhythmically waddle to the same beat? Have you ever called someone at home and the young person answers the phone with the same voice intonations as the parent? How does that happen?

It just does. You learn first by imitation, mirroring. Think about how you learned language. Your parents did not put grammar books in your crib, stating that they would be back in an hour for a short quiz! You watched them, heard them, and your brain recorded every piece of data and made it a part of you. It's how you learn foundationally. Discernments develop with age. Your first lessons were hand-me-downs, and for this discussion the focus is on Dads.

Until about the age of three, or when you became language literate, all Dad's stuff just got recorded in the mainframe of your computer brain. You probably had some inner dialogue, wrapped in amnesia. You probably said to yourself, "This is my Dad, male; this must be how men are, how they treat women, children, how they go to work, make money, talk, act, etc." You then incorporated these traits and gestures as your own to express yourself as a male, or the animus (male) aspects of self. It became your starter chip.

As you began to speak, you began to form more defined relationships. You could speak up, talk back, or say nothing, probably all triggered by what you witnessed from Dad's examples in relationships. You then experienced some kind of personal response. You felt good or bad, victim or controller, based on how you acted and the quality of the response. You watched Dad and Mom and made a special love-family chip. This chip became your hidden guidelines for the kind of relationships that you would attract later on.[18] Whether this was a good or not-so-good love-family chip, you were guaranteed to initially repeat it.

Often, by the time you are a young adult you have established aspects of Dad that you don't like, don't want to repeat. You have analyzed his behavior to some degree and have made some decisions about what hurt you, even

[18] Holmes, The Science of Mind, p. 222.

what may be incorrect for you. However, because all the Dad I-dents are programmed in, you are designed to behaviorally follow in his footsteps. If Dad yelled, you are more prone to yelling, or its direct opposite which just allows the "yelling" to stay buried inside, like combustible material. Either way, it's still yelling. This applies to other characteristics as well—alcohol, moods, affectionate displays, values toward people, money, God, success, government, and the dynamics of relationships.

These propensity chips are dominant in childhood. All feels normal then, even the undesirable. It is somewhere in the "Who am I?" of adolescence and young adulthood that your divided self begins to emerge. You don't often recognize it at first. It begins when you begin to desire and seek relationships, friends, boyfriends, girlfriends.

Your story may start as follows. You are with friends, male/female friends. It starts off great! You connect, you laugh, you bond. You may even be dating, falling in love. Then something happens. It just stops, perhaps due to a disagreement, a betrayal, someone moved, or you decided to like someone else. It created a conflict that in the big picture of your life may have been minor, but the process that it stirred from within was meant to be major. Because you probably lacked skillful awareness at that time, this major internal shift was left unnoticed. As a result you developed a shadow self. The shadow-you speaks softly in quiet moments about how you feel out of control, confused, as you are continuing in your adult relationship life. The shadow-self says, "Why do I do that? I thought it was the right thing to do? Or I guess this is just me, damaged goods?"

Oddly enough, the shadow-self is a natural part of the process of getting through to the Power of the inner archetype.[19] "Although our archetypal patterns are essentially neutral, they do have both light and shadow aspects. The word shadow itself suggests a dark, secretive, possibly malevolent countenance that looms in the background of our nature, ready to do harm to others as well as to ourselves. A much more appropriate understanding of the shadow aspects of our archetypes, however, is that they represent the part of our being that is least familiar to our conscious mind." Whether you use the shadow self, or allow it to use you, is determined again by your commitment to skillful awareness.

In your earlier days of love and relationships, it is reasonable that awareness wasn't available. As you came to feel this split, "Am I powerful or not? Am I right, important, recognized, appreciated or not?" the shadow-self became more formed and fed the paradoxical relationship to power itself. You became perhaps just as intimidated by being empowered as by being disempowered. Of course, it is easier to see why you would fear disempowerment. But why would you fear your real power? This is the core function of the shadow. The shadow is the unexplored you, and in your fear of the unknown you developed the art of sabotage. It then appears that you don't know why you do things you do, feel what you feel. This can become so painful that you feel a house divided, separating mind and heart.

---

[19] Holmes, The Science of Mind, 211.

Living with mind and heart divided is like having two battle encampments within, each one fighting for authority over power of choice. When isolated from each other, the heart and the mind are each handicapped; the mind tends to become hyper-rational, and the heart overly emotional. This imbalance of forces fragments our power. And like a nation in which opposing forces are constantly at war with each other, when our nature is fragmented it is vulnerable to being dominated by fear. As Jesus said, "If a kingdom is divided against itself, it cannot stand" (Mark 3:24).

This fear-dominated position directly influences all relationships. Your natural ability to be consistent in loving others (the light side of the Father Principle) is now greatly diminished by that fear and the robot-like behaviors programmed by the inappropriate Dad I-dents. At this point, you may feel your life's story is about to write the last chapter, entitled "What's the Use?" Just keep breathing; you are getting closer to your good news.

It is only when the head and heart don't have a clear channel of communication that you will remain confused about what you are doing in your life. The Prayer Room is the channel for this healing communication. The more you use it, the more you are able to understand what is really you as God created you, unique, individual, and designed for a purpose. Every prayerful inner entry will clear the darkened overlays of Dad's unresolved potential. You will then be able to stop projecting the confusion onto your relationships. Until this clarity occurs, it is likely that you will repeat at least in part some of the undesirable aspects that you absorbed from your father's relationship patterns.[20] This is what seems to make love hurt as you continue to grow in your relationship life. You are pained by your blind repetition of your wounded childhood experiences, by your choosing to do it over and over, by the unforgiven Dad I-dents that just seem to continue to rule you. "That suffering is actually a form of divine motivation, urging you to pursue a more authentic life."[21]

Regardless of the quality of any of your relationships—spouse, business partners, family, friends, children—all will be seen through the lens of a wounded self unless you initiate the healing. This is a huge decision and commitment, but the rewards are endless. Because of the Light Power of the Father Principle, as soon as you decide from within to deeply, truly change these false imprints, the Divine Illumination permanently embossed within you opens you to transcendent wisdom, healing, confidence, and joy. This Divine imprint is a universal contract for the real and can only be released by your wholehearted effort. "Whatever is Real cannot be threatened. Whatever is Unreal doesn't exist. Herein, lies the Peace of God."[22]

True relationships are love based, not fear based. This doesn't imply that an argument, upset, disappointment will never occur. It does mean that when it does, both of you, regardless of the kind of relationship, will have a clear channel to the TRUTH and that there will be NO lingering, painful residue, providing both are anchored to the Divine within. "For whatever is hidden is meant to be disclosed, and whatever is concealed is meant to be brought out into the open" (Mark 4:11, 21-22).

---

[20] Dan Kindlon, Ph.D., and Michael Thompson, Ph.D., Raising Cain (New York: Ballantine Books, 1999), 97.
[21] Holmes, The Science of Mind, p. 107.
[22] Inner Peace Foundation, A Course in Miracles (Farmingdale, NY: Coleman, 1975), 1.

Prepare now for a particular Prayer Room exercise designed to illuminate any hidden projection patterns that you may have in your relationships with loved ones, family, friends, colleagues.

Prayer Room Exercise: Illuminate Hidden Projection Patterns

- Allow yourself to be comfortable and quiet for awhile, and enter into your Prayer Room as outlined in Chapter One.

- Allow yourself to be in your Prayer Room and continue to relax more deeply by taking slow and deep breaths.

- Now allow your mind to play back an image of any particular relationship that you willfully choose to change, to heal, that is not your father.

- Watch the memory, like a movie on a wide video screen.

- Notice everything between you and the other person—gestures, tone of voice, verbal interactions, win/lose games, power plays, push-pull feelings.

- Now imagine you can split the screen, and the right side is now viewing this present relationship while the left side is viewing a memory from your childhood including some interaction with Dad, Mom, you.

- Again, notice everything.
  - How did you feel back then—loved, safe, neglected, silenced?
  - Were you favored? Criticized? Ignored by Dad?
  - What did you do to get Dad's attention?
  - Were you hugged? Paid attention to?

- When did you see Dad? Day, night, often, or not?
- What did you do with your father? What activities, play, traditions did you or didn't you have with him?
- How did he treat your mother?
- Did they love each other? How did they show it? Or why didn't they love each other and how was that lack of love demonstrated?
- Was your father active in your life, school, friends, events? How did this make you feel?
- Can you recall a very important experience that left a deep positive/negative impression?
- Do you know how your father felt about God, prejudice, money, sex, government, authority?
- Do you remember your Dad laughing, crying, sad, worried, loving, angry?
- Can you see any of these characteristic impressions from childhood being replayed by you or the other person?
- If so, does it make you feel stuck, not free in this present relationship?
- Do you know how to change the undesirable influences in this present relationship without using fear, anger, control, manipulation?
- Are you really ready to change all projections in this relationship in order to experience whatever is REAL between you?
- If so, repeat slowly and with conviction these affirmations:
    - I am willing to see the Truth in this relationship.
    - I release my fears, and the projections onto [name] that my

fears have created.

- I choose to be honest in myself and ask the Divine Father Light to show me all patterns of jealousy, false expectation, and dependency that do not serve the Highest Good between us.

- I ask my Divine Father Light to dissolve all these useless patterns at their causal moment, so that I can re-create love patterns instead.

- I ask my Divine Father Light to show me with a bright light of discernment all that may be limiting my real ability to love and be loved, as it refers to what I may have inherited from my father.

- I ask my Divine Father Light to infuse me with the discipline, strength, courage, joy, and self-love necessary to re-create all my relationships to healthy, mutually respectful experiences, or to set them free.

- I now and always choose to stay anchored in the Light of my Divine Father Love to remove all personal labels, i.e., "Daddy's Little Girl," "favorite son/daughter," "Princess," "Prince," so that I can just be me ... as God intended me to be.

- Take your time with each affirmation, even repeat each one three times for better comprehension.

- When you are done, slowly ascend the Golden Light steps back out to outer consciousness.

It is highly suggested that you repeat this exercise many times. Each time you will gain more insight. Also, write out each affirmation and repeat each one ten times daily for one month for best results.

Chapter Six: Parenting With or Without Children

There is no greater cause, no greater purpose, no greater gift to the planet than children. They are simultaneously our promise for a better tomorrow and the legacy of our unresolves.

I began to see this glaring contradiction in the early days of my professional career. I was an English teacher in Barringer High School, Newark, New Jersey. I began teaching at the end of the Newark riots. My kids obviously had to be more focused on survival than parts of speech. I saw their gaping wounds of fear, personal insecurity, and the desperate need to be coached out of their seeming no-hope life cycles, all neatly wrapped in a tough, I dare you to attitude. I learned more from them than they will ever know!

Unless the core heart and soul of a child is nurtured and safe, the mind remains chained, blocked, subject to behavioral atrocities, unable to explore its true potential. These inner shackles will remain so until somewhere, somehow children are shown the pathway to their own inner talents and ultimate self-reliance. The present condition concerning children in our society proves this has not been accomplished. The news is filled with everyday accounts of missing children, violence, kids shooting kids, date rape, excessive use of drugs and alcohol. And the most devious demon today, that clearly rivets me in emotional pain and frustration, is the ongoing, terrifying rise in child pornography. There is no wound deeper, no damage more severe, that so splinters the spirit, than child abuse. It is the total abomination of the purity of the Father Principle. "What loving father would give his son stone, when he asked for bread?"

These wounds are the responsibility of all adults regardless of whether each is a parent or not. All children have inherited our stuff. Relying on the Light of the Father Principle in all its inherent gifts of orderliness, stability, responsibility, cause and effect, proper boundaries, respect, honor protection, and the promise that life is good, MUST be exemplified through all adults. When this promise is kept, it becomes the living proof of the Father Principle (cause and effect) because it heals both the giver and the receiver, both the adult and the child.

Not releasing the promise of Father Power is evident in what now appears normal in some families. Families now are commonly suffering from the ills of divorce, separation, loss of father physically, emotionally, due to long work hours, too much time spent in front of some kind of a screen—TV, PC, DVD—instead of a person, lack of good routines in family activities, such as meals, chores, bedtime, and family-together time. Alcohol, drugs, domestic violence, and ongoing parent-child numb silence may be witnesses as part of everyday family life. Stress within the family, arguing, financial problems, unhappy spousal relationships, and kids ruling parents through anger, tantrums, and material neediness could be an easy script for any TV sitcom or movie.

The real problem with all of this is not the problems themselves but that families seem not to move more consistently to live in their solutions. I believe this is so because most people have not gone deep enough into Self to find the healing wisdom from within the Father Creator Light. You may see this in your own family. It may appear to you that your family situations can only get somewhat improved. You are correct. As long as those involved stay with an external locus of focus, it is not likely to improve. Circumstances don't change. Thoughts, feelings must change and then the behavior to follow will be altered.

Whether you are a parent or not, it is important and necessary for the sake of all that you change your attitude about your influence on all children. First you need to remember all children learn best by example. Your children are watching everything about you. They are thirsty for the truth that will prove to be durable when they are adults. Say what you mean; mean what you say to them.

There is no time off as a parent. Parenting is the hardest, most significant "job" on the planet. Parents are the very extensions of God's hands. As an adult, you are shaping the future, today, through how you relate to your children. They so need you; they so want to be with you. It is instinctual. Children are totally dependent on you initially for everything. This can be an insurmountable daily climb if the parent is not rooted from within.

Your children cannot anchor to you if you are unanchored. They will seek elsewhere. They will create a substitute family safety somewhere. They will go out into the world unskilled in discernment and probably attach to something or someone that may feel good and may not be good for them.

This family safety needs to be created as early as possible. However, regardless of what the family dynamics may be, the light from within is ageless, timeless, and ever-available for you to choose and use to re-create a better family.

There must be family guidelines. Essential to this are mealtime and bedtime, which establish a rhythm which lets children know they are a part of the community called family. It teaches them to relate, to communicate, whether it looks like they like it or not.

Mealtime was always a big deal in my house. It still is. We would have dinner together every night, no matter what. We would not eat until my father came home. It was a routine. Dad would come in and we were to be ready, table set, and then we would say "Grace" (we each had a turn) and then begin our meal. We would stay at the table for at least an hour. Dad would ask us questions about the day, decisions would be discussed, and absolutely we were NOT allowed to speak on the phone during dinner. If someone did call, my father would answer the phone and say, "Yes, how are you? Ginger is having dinner now and she will see you in school tomorrow." I would barely blink during those moments.

Now, I know you may think this is "corny," too severe, very fifties, or very Sicilian. You may be correct in all of it. But let me share how this translated into my heart and adult personality. I was sure we were a family. Family came first. Respecting our private time was a given. I was wanted as a member of my family. There were rules to respect and rules kept everyone safe. Authority was good if it was intended for the good. My father wanted to be with us, and he was to be in charge of creating our world and then to release me from it strong enough to make my own.

Does this sound too perfect? It wasn't. We had lots of family problems. We just learned to solve them, no matter how long it took. My father and my mother were, and still are, very prayerful people. We would always acknowledge that being close to God was staying close to everything that is good, happy, healing, truthful. Sound too corny again? Truthfully, it doesn't matter how it sounds. I know it worked. Dad created a household that was real. He would cry, laugh, get mad; kiss my mother, kiss us; repeatedly tell us, "Money doesn't grow on trees"; ground me for broken rules; get to know all my friends, scrutinize all my boyfriends; ask a million questions—"Where are you going?" "How are you getting there?" "Be home on time or else." There were times when I thought all of this was just awful. But my father always told me the truth and his whole life is a trophy example of that. That kind of integrity shaped me, reshaped, and continues to shape me. It made all the difference in the world. Through his example, I could go out into the world and trust myself to create my own success.

The world and families are certainly different now than in the 1950s. Some changes have propelled us into becoming a better humanitarian global family. Other changes have deepened the separation between head and heart and have made it harder for us to balance a progressive life while attempting to get back to basics. Perhaps the answer lies in bringing forward the kernel of simplicity from the past and weaving it into the technological demands of daily living. Again, a safe home and family are the core for such stability.

Have more family meals. Everyone needs to participate, have chores, and keep their word. Shut off the electronic noise! Sit with your kids. Tell them stories about when you were a kid. Show them old photos while you are telling your stories. Right now your kids only know you as an adult. They need to see the cause and effect of your life by you explaining what happened in your life as a kid with your parents and grandparents. Tell them the truth. Tell them when you were afraid, embarrassed, hurt, or disappointed. Tell them how you resolved it, what you learned from it. Tell them how you felt to be in love. They need to hear it from you, or their needs will push them into people and places that are not so trustworthy. If they hear and know the truth about life, emotions, ups and downs from you, they have a much better chance of acting out of that truth when they are not with you. Pray with your kids. If you personally are still unresolved by God, Universal Divine, faith, go and figure it out! Don't leave your kids confused about the most beautiful, powerful, Law of Love, God. Learn with them.

47

Question everything. Seek truth, love, the Divine from within. Learn to trust your silence, your prayers, and your kids will do the same.

Make ample time every day to talk to everyone in your immediate family. Write happy, "I'm proud of you; I love you" notes and put them in your kids' lunches and underwear drawers! Do the same for your spouse or partner. Everyone needs a daily dose of "I love you." Celebrate often with your family, for the little things and the big things. Make a special meal because someone got a home run or got a higher grade. Make cookies together. Have fun making a mess and then clean it up together. Paint your kids' rooms together. Do family projects together, clean the basement or garage, etc., then plan some kind of celebration together. Stop all the useless running around, everyone going in separate directions, not knowing what anyone is doing.

Put your children in charge of certain responsibilities (age appropriate) and reward them by telling them, in front of everyone, how much you really appreciate them for doing that particular chore. Let them know they are making the family work better because of it. Let them know you need their talents to help you learn more about life!

Be more affectionate to each other for no reason. Families at times can become very out of touch with one another. Get involved in your children's interests. Ask them to talk about why they like something. Take your children on family outings to show them different aspects of life. Get involved in volunteer projects with them. Take the toys they no longer want and go with them to give the toys to various children's organizations so that they can see not everyone lives the same way.

Let your children see you reading. Read to them more. Even if they are older, if you find an article that teaches you something, read at least a portion of it to them, then leave it for them to finish.

Play pretend games with your kids. It's fun, free, and opens everyone's imagination. Play pretend, like you are a ---------- and then fill in the blank with an occupation and a made-up story that could go with it. This is great while driving with your children and very stimulating for what they could be.

If you have little ones, my suggestion is to get them out of your bed. It ruins your intimacy. It also tells your children that you and your spouse don't have a private time. This is not a good boundary. If a child is not feeling well or is upset, go into the child's room to comfort him or her. Tell your child stories about angels and happy endings that will soothe him or her back to sleep.

If you don't have children of your own, get involved in a child's life more directly. They need you and vice versa. Nieces, nephews, grandchildren, neighbors' kids all need adults whom their parents can trust. Parenting is too big a job, too complex to be only the work of one mother and one father. Besides, children need the diversification of personalities to better shape and determine their own. Please be aware that being involved with a child does not always have to involve spending money on him or her. Spend time with the child.

The dividends are for all involved. If there are older generations still present in your family, this is a real blessing. Kids need to respect the experiences of the elderly and to learn again the cause and effect of a life and how it was lived. Kids really are naturally compassionate. Hatred, anger, selfishness are imitated aspects of personality. When children are around the elderly naturally, it won't take long before some kind of loving gesture or experience is exchanged. Even if a kid lives next to some grumpy old man whose only comment is "Get off my property," with your proper explanation a lesson of love and compassion can be learned.

Parents, adults, and children are the formational foundation for all relationships. This is how you got to be who you are today. Whatever might have been missed when you were a child can be reclaimed by giving to a child. You need children as much as they need you.

Let us prepare for a specific healing Prayer Room exercise now designed to enhance and correct parent-child relationships.

Prayer Room Exercise:
Who Are You as Parent?

- Allow yourself to be comfortable and quiet for awhile and follow the ritual for entering into your Prayer Room as outlined in Chapter One.
- Take a few deep breaths and relax, filling yourself, surrounding yourself with the Blue White Light that is pouring into your Prayer Room from the skylight above you.
- Now relax and again repeat a few times the word "Peace, Peace, Peace."
- Allow yourself to feel; trust your first impressions as you respond to the following questions:

- Who are you as a parent, grandparent, aunt, uncle, etc. as you relate to children?
- Are you the controller? Do you find yourself afraid of their creativity, their energy?
- Do you think your position with them is to do what you say while you still don't follow your own good advice?
- What is your tone of voice with kids?
- Do you really listen to them, respect them?
- Are you always telling them something they have to do, without spending real time talking with them? Do you look at them directly in their eyes while speaking?
- Does one of your children fit the squeaky wheel example?
- How did she/he get that way?
- Do you play with your kids, laugh, cry, pray with your kids? Why or why not?
- Do you express your feelings about life to your kids?
- How do you answer questions from your kids about God, sex, violence, drugs, alcohol, fear, money?
- What gets triggered in you when you do?
- Do you say please, thank you, I love you to one another often, daily? Why or why not?
- Do you attach yourself to one of your children in such a way that it is as if he/she becomes your emotional surrogate spouse?
- If your children were to describe you, what would they say?
- Be relaxed and take a few more deep breaths, and while imagining a

picture of everyone in your family, repeat the following, calling each by name, then saying:

- I love you; I promise to be more open with you, more honest, more available.

- I love you; I am sorry if I really didn't listen to you when you were wanting to tell me what was really going on for you.

- I love you; I forgive you for not being there for me when I might have needed you to be.

- I love you; I promise to know you more, laugh with you more, trust you more by trusting me, and God within me, to help us all to be a closer family.

- I love you; I promise to change me more as an example for you to do the same.

- I love you; I'm sorry if some of my habits have hurt you—smoking, drinking, drugs, anger, violence, non-communication, depression, control patterns.

- I love you; I promise to change these habits because I know it will heal the whole family.

- I love you; I desire for you to talk to me more, be with me more because it heals me, teaches me.

- I love you; I love you; I ask Father God Light to directly heal ----- (then name each one) in the best way, fastest way that serves the whole family.

- Then relax, breathe again, repeating "Peace, Peace, Peace."
- Then say "Thank you" and come back up the ten ascending Golden

Light steps and back out to outer awareness.

It is suggested that you write feelings in your journal. Repeat this exercise once weekly to keep family in a forward healing. All is possible for those who believe!

Chapter Seven : Parenting Your-Self

A clear illustration of a splintered Father Principle is that you probably don't follow your own good advice. The Light side of the Father Power seems to become very functional for you whenever you make recommendations for others and help them solve their issues; yet there are times when you don't do the same for yourself. Somehow you manage to block that Light when it comes to using it for yourself. This split occurs because you haven't spent enough quiet time in yourself, for yourself. Part of this may stem from a hand-me-down attitude that said if you focused on you getting better it would be a selfish need. That would be like saying it's better to breathe in than out! Loving yourself is loving others. You can't give what you don't have.

Helping yourself, re-creating yourself is the best thing you could do for you and those you love. Unfortunately, you may only be triggered to improve or finally feel safe enough to improve due to some personal crisis. Then it's as if that crisis gave you a license to at last do it for you.

No matter what your values, beliefs, thoughts, feelings are, you become them. If you believe that personal inner evolvement is good, you become that. If you believe that you are supposed to take care of others, manage the house, the kids, the college fund, the yard, the Christmas Club, and all the family matters before you get to you, chances are you have lost your-Self along the way; and you probably have trained everyone around you that "You'll take care of it" and your own needs don't really matter.

The truth is that if you were more inwardly secure and aware you might have shaped some decisions differently, and might have been able to demonstrate this skillful awareness to others in your family. This would have eliminated some issues and would have created a better-balanced, interdependent family. Regardless of the could have, should have, would have, all of us become our self-fulfilling prophecies, both positive and negative. This too is an expression of the Father Principle in its cause and effect relationship of thoughts creating situations.

Because this is a Universal Law, you can lawfully step in and use it anytime. It's never too late. It begins with you and the decision to go for it.

Many issues arise when you don't understand that you were designed to eventually parent, father yourself. Some behavioral issues that are demonstrated as a result of the unparented self are continuous procrastination, problems with authority, repeated misguided career choices, 'poor-loser' attitudes, chronic unpaid debts, misuse of credit cards, hot-tempered outbursts of anger that over-dramatize, chronic lateness, inability to keep commitments to self and others, holding a grudge, gambling, and a lack of being a self-starter.

These behavioral symptoms become your actions out of a blind awareness. You don't or can't see the consequences these actions will have. The unparented self ultimately acts in childish ways. One very chronic display of the unparented person is staying an emotional victim. Disappointment, hurt, betrayal, untimely death, loss of love are just as much a part of life as achievement, promotion, recognition, and finding your true soul mate. But staying bolted to "Why did this happen to me?" is a major cause of what I call power leakage.

Many times a victimizing circumstance will occur and you may think you have dealt with it completely. The dangerous power leakage happens, however, when you don't thoroughly let go of the emotions attached to that situation. You bury them, thinking, "What else was I supposed to do?" Days, weeks, months, even years go by and suddenly something someone does or says that may have nothing to do with you at the time, but may be similar in its theme, can send you into a tailspin of emotion, putting you right back into the time it happened to you. This is a true indication that you aren't over it and the residues of emotions are still in charge of you.

Chronic power leakage happens in everyone. It is the result of living without the full power of real self from within. Without full knowledge and skill to continuously release the Father Light whenever you need it, you're basically just stuck with the past repeatedly re-creating itself into your future.

The Father Light is Creator Light. When you regularly tap into the Wisdom Well, you are guaranteed a new creative ending for the old, and a new creative beginning that promises to heal and seal chronic power leakage.

The eighties and nineties were filled with the buzz of codependency. It was described as attaching one's self to a person, place, or substance, and giving it a meaning that it didn't have. For example, "You're my everything, my whole life; my job, my home is my life; I don't know what I would do if I couldn't smoke, drink, do drugs, shop, spend money." All these statements stab your spirit and leave you spilling the fear of what if? in everything you do. I do think we are all codependent to a greater or lesser degree because we have in some way put the Source of our Power outside and in a certain person, place, or thing. We make the person, place, or thing God and become a little more powerless every day. Parenting yourself calls back that power and makes you whole again.

Because some of these victim life events are old, the guilt, depression, shame, anger, resentment, fear that has been stored can be very deep. You need a daily M.A.P. to be your strategy for changing you from feelings of powerlessness in motion into power in action. M.A.P. is daily meditation, affirmation, and prayer.

Meditation is using your Prayer Room on a regular basis, and doing the exercises as they have been outlined. Affirmation is the repetition of positive power statements. These power sentences are to be repeated while you are in your Prayer Room so that your inner conscious self can absorb them and then allow them to become a natural part of your behavior patterns. You also need to write them daily. Writing affirmations and saying them daily is a needed reinforcement to keep your mind on this new desired track. Affirmations do the same for your belief systems that braces do for your teeth. Affirmations retrain your thoughts and your energy to move in a more suitable direction. You also need to pay attention to your language patterns. The way you speak is a result of the way you think. Big, red flags go up when someone has certain language habits. Verbal phrases like, "I'm used to not having it work out; I don't trust easily; I can't afford it; I've always been this way; not at my age; I forgive but I don't forget; no one listens to me; it will never get any better," are examples of these red flags. These are bold declarations to make about yourself that stunt your potential for happiness and success. Pay attention to what you say. Practice making a picture of everything you say, whether it's to yourself or out loud. Look at what you are saying about yourself. If that picture doesn't really express a self-confident, self-respecting you, then change your words immediately. Sometimes what you say is a subconscious blurting out of an old wound. When you change your words on the spot, you startle your library of the mind into rewriting some of its volumes. This thought interruption will so impress you, you can even feel an increase of energy in that very moment. With that second look, you will have sealed up more power leakage.

You will need to pray every day. Prayer is a conversation with the Divine Light. Sometimes you are requesting. And sometimes you are listening for deeper insight. It's important to do both. Another level of prayer is silence while resting in your Prayer Room. You need to do this also. The more you spend time inside, quietly, the more the useless, idle chatter of worry and negativity will stop. Since no two things can occupy the same space at the same time and since the Creator Light Power from within is the greatest Power of all Life, your mind chatter will come up, burn off, and stop. Then you are ready to really hear the Voice of Silence as a Creator God who is always there, always ready to direct you, heal you. This Silence has to be practiced because most of your life is usually so mentally noisy. Start with just being in your Prayer Room for five minutes and do nothing. Even if you are uncomfortable, just keep doing five minutes daily, then increase it, until you are successful at just being quiet and listening deep inside yourself for about twenty minutes. The results are amazing. Typically, most of what you thought was a problem will have faded away. You will notice you are more open to innovative urges that redirect your present plans into a more productive end.

The more you rely on the Light inside, the less you can be pulled off your center of True Self, jarred by others' opinions and negativity. Staying grounded in a world filled with blurring upsets, worry, injustice, prejudice, and terrorism is a real asset. It makes you the asset. You can now parent yourself into safety, patience, compassion, because you are not solely dependent on persons, places, and things to maintain your happiness and self-worth. You begin to really enjoy your own company.

You may think this self-reliance and ongoing resourcefulness leads to self-isolation. On the contrary, you become very attractive. Your energy becomes inviting to others because you are good, free, and have less baggage.

Being resourceful in this context means re (going back) source (to the Source) ful (completely). The resourcefulness of your True Self allows you to be clear minded and parallels you with the Divine Mind. In this, the help you may need (person, place, thing) feels more like inspired decisions and choices. A Divine synchronicity occurs when you least expect it.

You then attract others of your same vibration to be around you. Since you are now more connected to the Divine Mind from within, you create Divine Right Actions in your environment. You live a higher quality of life because your inner connection dictates it to be so.

This Source of All is always within you. Relying on it, feeling it to be as close as a loving father and child changes your life dramatically. You ironically can feel really in charge of your life, your self. You know that there is a part of you, inside, that is trustworthy, consistent, and all-knowing. It is the Father Creator who purposefully designed you in His Image.

Let us prepare to go into the Prayer Room to clear away hidden beliefs and language patterns that are keeping you childish instead of childlike and creative.

(i.e., assertiveness, independence, responsibility, commitment, reputation) and towards men in general. As discussed in Chapter Two, this is the normal mix, like flint against stone that was meant to spark you into a deeper understanding of the Father Principle in its spiritual causal dimension.

Some use these early experiences to spur them on to personal evolution. And some become emotionally lazy and just recycle the Dad I-dents on to the next generation. These individuals live, work, play within the boundaries of both positive and negative aspects of their Dad chips. They stay within these limits through fear and a lack of awareness and motivation. Their lives look normal and may even be measurably successful. But they will always have that blind spot about their own reality, never really certain about their true personal power. I would say, unfortunately, that much of our society "camps out" in that last description.

With this mixed set of messages, you can live out your life with a veiled sense about why you are in the career path you're in, whether you really fear God, love God, are angry at God, or just don't know who or what God is. You can continue to make a home, family, and all its traditions, but still have a part of you that fades out at family celebrations while continuing to go through the motions that seem at the time to be necessary and/or important. Occasionally, you may allow yourself to daydream a different life, silencing yourself from acknowledging unfinished desires and unfortunate regrets. You may feel trapped by temper tantrums, depression, poor money habits, intimacy issues, sexual inhibitions, alcoholism, and biological predispositions.

All of these, to name a few, are common assumptions for struggling and maintaining a status quo energy-engine as you move on from year to year. Occasionally, bonuses, vacations, a "fling," or keeping those ten pounds off longer than expected create a temporary breakthrough that is just that— temporary.

These are the common wounds, commonly left unhealed, that manifest a fairly good and somewhat satisfying life, even though there is the dull pain of lingering Dad I-dents.

But the most dangerous disruptions to the natural ability for a happy life are the Dad I-dents that violated your soul. Any experience between you and any dynamic with your father or father-figure type that distorted your ability to trust what is innately good and loving is a crime against your spirit for natural piety. These crimes, unfortunately, have become common. Witnessing domestic violence or being sexually and/or physically abused always leaves your soul fractured.

Your own wounds may be deep wounds, caused by broken trust. Divorce, infidelity, abandonment, drugs, alcohol, anger, lack of affection are all deep wounds. Deep wounds leave deep openings. And again, you can allow these chasms to drain your life force away or you can go into them deeper and deeper, until you find their buried gifts. The tools necessary for this plunge are patience, Prayer Room exercises, a real commitment to get to the bottom of it all, in some cases professional counseling, and a new definition of forgiveness.

So often you hear, "I forgive, but I don't forget." This has nothing to do with real forgiveness. This is a grudge and a concealed weapon to be used at a later time. For some, never forgiving, keeping the rage and pain, makes them think they are holding a claim ticket for justice. They're not. The only things they are holding onto are toxicity and the promise for damaged cell tissue and dis-ease.

This is not to suggest that forgiveness of anything, to anyone, is easy. It is not. True forgiveness is not an action or statement. It is a process that can take a long time to completion.

Let us examine the full process of forgiveness in all its stages. Firstly, there is an event or experience that, at that moment, hurt you. If may have even shocked you. You were wounded, stabbed by a betrayal, neglect, abandonment, death, divorce, rejection, rape, or any act of violence. Your entire being absorbed this experience. Regardless of whether it occurred to you physically, emotionally, financially, mentally, or spiritually, it happened to you. All of you felt it, with or without awareness. The deeper the blow, the more of a shock it was to your whole person. If the experience was ongoing, it probably kept your vitality for life in shock. You became slightly numb for a long time. In repeated abuse situations, this defense of numb increases into disassociation. When you have the same wound over and over, you miraculously find a way to psychologically not feel like you are in your body, so that you literally don't have to feel anything anymore. The fear of when it will happen again becomes so great that it is just easier to shut off feelings altogether. This is an example of a truly fractured soul.

The next stage is to bury the real account of the experience into the library of the mind. The event gets vaulted but not the emotional vulnerability that it created. Your emotional wounds shadow over your consciousness like a surface abrasion. You may have called getting this surface abrasion bumped, "he/she pushed my buttons." This brings us to the next stage. We will project onto others what is really our causal wound, not a new abrasion being caused by others.

A typical display of such a projection can be seen in the course of meeting a new friend, lover, employee, employer, neighbor, etc. At the beginning of the relationship, there is a kind of click chemistry. You just get along. You then pursue a relationship. You share time, ideas, celebrations. It all seems to be going along just great. And then a conflict occurs. A disagreement or argument or the like occurs that breaks the bliss. Your outer consciousness mind may blame the other person, or be confused by the disappointment. You will analyze it and figure out what was their "wrong" and maybe what was yours.

You will then perhaps go to the other person to seek resolve. This may oftentimes just stir up an even greater conflict because the other person doesn't see it the way you do. Here comes more upset, more drama, disappointment, and anger, and less discussion that would lead to a peaceful end. At this point, the unaware person can further bury real feelings, assuming the two just won't ever be able to see eye-to-eye. There now exists a shadow limitation between you. Some will say it is like the elephant in the room that no one is talking about. At this point, the relationship may become status quo, drift apart, or become chronically explosive.

Unless you pursue the true cause of the upset at its source, it is predictable that you will create it again. The inward pursuit is what shifts the awareness from that surface bruise to the origin of pain that was experienced much earlier in life and has remained unattended to. This contradiction of inside source pain and outer abrasions in relationships is your soul urging you to heal the way nature intended, from inside out. The urging is what is pushing out familiar feelings and situations from the past so that you, hopefully, can't leave them unhealed. This is the function of projection.

The old wounds have grown adhesions over your eyes, making you unable to see the complete present truth in any given situations, which now further complicates why both parties may not see eye to eye (I to I ... ego to ego). Your perception (adhesions) creates your projection. This is also accurately viewed from the cliché statement, "I took it out on him/her." Literally you took a photo memory, similar to the original wound, and superimposed it over the person. You took a reminiscent feeling out of you and draped it on him/her, suggesting it was his/her problem.

It is vital to note that projection is almost unavoidable and can be your greatest gift. Once you can recognize this part of the process of forgiveness, you can then go on to the next powerful stage. Having the clues presented in the projection, you can then realize that perhaps this conflict has readied you to heal at a deeper level.

There will always be similar upset feelings in the outer conflict that were equal to the causal wound. This next step is clearly up to you. If you go inside (Prayer Room) and carefully, with spiritual illumination, examine how does this represent a scene from my earlier days? (and in this discussion pertinent to father dynamics), you will then be able to reframe the conflict in your world. It now becomes a gift to heal what was buried. Until you remember the painful blind spots, they will continue to hurt you. Because of this, there is great power in remembering. Hopefully, this recalling will spark you to forgive the surface conflict, since you are now aware of your projections. Your only concern for true forgiveness is your projection. As you forgive those who offended you and those whom you have offended (all this can effectively be done in your Prayer Room), you will realize that without this outer conflict you may never have had the opportunity to get to the bottom of it. This event, then, can become a glorious release for you. You are no longer in the bondage of your own past. You are set free to be more completely you, no longer chained with one foot in the past. The point of power is always in the present. At any single moment, you, by your own decision, can release this suppressed scarring. It is really up to you and then the Power within you will begin to heal you!

True forgiveness is a gift you give yourself. Should you decide to forgive in this process manner, you will have dissolved the button, and the likelihood of that chronic conflict occurring again is eradicated.

What remains then is the original wound that was so deep between you and Dad. You may be thinking How do I eliminate that? Honestly, it is a matter of how willing you are to trust the Spiritual Essence of the Father Principle and the truth of its ultimate connection to the Father Creator, God.

Sometimes this point of your deep inner healing can feel like a "Catch 22." Many times father wounds have been projected onto the face of God the Father, making complete healing seem impossible. Healing of this kind is a matter of your choice and your pace. Draw to you the portion you are ready for. Even if you begin with the basic decision to no longer be

70

under the effect of the past, you are a winner! Eventually, through your pure intentionality and consistent efforts, you will feel and experience the Permanent Template of Father Light in its truth—that is, Peace, Love, and Abundance.

You can begin with the simple conviction to use the hurtful experience as shear motivation to claim your victory and maybe even help others in the process. Your original pain then becomes your personal platform for empowerment! You will have changed the course of your life merely by this decision alone! You can heal. You need to decide to! The Universal Law of the Creator within you will continue to carry you through to completion.

The deepest scars can serve a great purpose. Given that you can't change what did happen, only how you feel about it, you can stay in charge by assigning new feelings to this experience. Only you can choose your feelings. You are more equipped to choose your feelings now, certainly, than as a vulnerable child. Choose again. Choose now to use the pain to recreate your life the way you desire to be, not as it was mandated by the experience. Choose again. Choose now. Do it for those you love. You are greater from "the Within" than you realize. Remember to use your M.A.P. as described in an earlier chapter. Daily, sometimes hourly, remember the God signature that is always inside you and write a new script for your life! This is real evolution. I believe we are designed to "outdo" our parents. We are designed to go forward, know more, heal more, love more, forgive more, be more.

All children deserve to see adults as examples of hope. It is how you can use your pain as a legacy of love.

As a Christian, I have spent much time seeking deeper meaning and values from the life of the Rabbi Jesus. I seek to know and share the legacy of His experiences. In the last hour of His life, broken and emptied of even His life force blood (it is recorded that when Jesus was pierced in His side, there was only water left to flow out of His body), He cried out to His Father, "Father, forgive them, for they know not what they do."

My own reflection of this, as it applies to our personal lives, is that when someone wounds you, at some level that person is not knowing of his/her true Spirit-Self; someone probably splintered his/her soul as well. That person also doesn't know and is not in control of what you <u>do</u> with that wound. You at any moment can free yourself from the crosses that you've carried. Your truth will set you free. Forgive other people as soon as possible.

Let us prepare for two Prayer Room exercises. The first one is to help heal and forgive conflicts caused by projection. The second one will be to help heal the original father wound.

Prayer Room Exercise A: Projection

- Allow yourself to relax and follow the ritual for entering into the Prayer Room as outlined in Chapter One.
- Take a few deep breaths and repeat silently, "Peace, Peace, Peace."
- Continue to fill yourself completely with the Blue White Light that is cascading in through the skylight overhead.
- Just relax and allow yourself to respond to the following questions,

openly and honestly.

- Select a recent conflict in your life, with family, partner, spouse, or someone at work.
- Review the conflict while you are in your Prayer Room as if you were watching it on a large video screen.
- Observe all the body language of everyone involved, especially your own.
- Hear the dialogue that occurred during this recent conflict.
- Recall your feelings during the conflict.
  - What did you feel: anger, sadness, fear, disappointment, rejection, insecurity, unjust criticism, blame, guilt, manipulation, deceit?
  - Go into these feelings now as deeply as you can.
  - Where do you feel these feelings? In your head, heart, stomach?
  - What does this remind you of? When did you have these feelings as a child?
  - How did these feelings get triggered when you were a child?
  - Did it involve any dynamic between you and your father or father-type?
  - Are you willing to see this outer conflict as a reflection from some unresolved earlier wound?
  - Can you see how this is a projection from the past onto the present?
  - Are you willing to forgive and release all negative feelings pertinent to this outer conflict? Are you willing to see how your past wound made you vulnerable to this kind of a conflict?

    – Are you willing to rely on the Father Creator Light to clear any false perceptions so that you can stop the past from repeating itself?

- Now take a deep breath and allow the Blue White Light from above to continuously flow through you and around you as you repeat several times:

  - Father Creator, Light of Truth and Love, cleanse me of all false perceptions and illusions about this conflict [name it]. Release me from my fears and insecurities caused by early wounds and show me the truth lesson that my soul wants me to learn through this conflict.

- Relax, again repeating silently, "Peace, Peace, Peace."

- Then be still and trust your first impressions; it will give you insight as to the real cause of this outer conflict.

- Take your time.

- Then ask,

  - Father, Creator, Light of Truth and Love, show me the best solution that is based on the highest good for all concerned."

- Relax, again be still and trust your first impressions; it will guide you to a proper solution.

- It is now your choice to decide to follow these insights to the proper solution.

- Relax, take a deep breath again and say,

  - Father Creator, Light of Truth and Love, thank you for this healing and insightful guidance. I will (or not) take this action to create a peace resolve.

Prayer Room Exercise B:
Healing the Original Father Wound

- Enter into your Prayer Room as outlined in Chapter One.
- Take your time and take several deep breaths. Repeat silently, "Peace, Peace, Peace."
- Relax and fill yourself completely with the Blue White Light pouring through the skylight above you.
- Now take three slow, deep breaths and say,
    - Oh, Angels of Wisdom and Peace, come and be with me now, as I desire to heal all the pain and all negative effects that may have been created between me and my father.
- Relax and allow the Angel of Wisdom to be on one side of you and the Angel of Peace to be on the other side of you.
- You may take a moment now and ask their names, if you choose to.
- With your Angels there now to protect and guide you, ask them to bring the image of your father onto your wide video screen (it doesn't matter if your father is deceased).
- Take your time and just observe him—facial expressions, clothes.
- Take your time, relax, and totally focus on your feelings. Pay attention to everything you feel.
- Allow for all emotions, without judging any of them.
- You are safe with your Angels; they continuously protect you; you can

ask them any questions you desire.

- Now breathe deeply and ask,

  - Oh, Angels of Wisdom and Peace, show me the truth about the wounds I experienced from my father.

- Then just relax and trust your FIRST impressions.

- Remember your Angels are there guiding, directing, and protecting. They will keep you surrounded in a shield of Blue White Light throughout this healing.

- Now ask your Angels to open your awareness to show you how you can use this wound to strengthen you; ask what is your greater lesson that can spur you on to personal victory and greatness.

- Just relax and take your time. Feel all emotions and accept all insights, even if at the moment you seem not to understand.

- Now follow your Angels, as they will place you on an examining table that is in the center of your Prayer Room.

- Your Angels will now remove all toxic residue that may be lingering in your whole being, physically, emotionally, financially, mentally, and spiritually. They will move their hands all "through" your body and pull out what may appear as "grey dust." Then they will transform the grey dust into glittering sparkles and cause it to disappear.

- You will sense them saying to you, "Dear One, you are a child of God, now and always. You hold within you the breath of Creator Light. No one can ever take that away from you, NO MATTER WHAT. We are your Healing Messengers and we will continue to restore you to your full potential, as God intended, because you asked. Peace, now, Dear

One, feel your Healing Peace."

- Take your time—do not rush through this! Relax as long as you desire to do so.

- When you are ready, silently repeat

    - Peace, Peace, Peace. I release all these wounds and all their negative effects now. I release you, father, to the Creator so that you may be healed as well. We are no longer in bondage because of any harmful experiences. All is forgiven and released. Only the Peace, Truth, Love, Healing of God remains. It is done now. Thank you, Angels. Thank you, God. Amen, Amen, Amen.

It is suggested that you repeat this exercise as often as desired and needed. It may be helpful to record in a journal so you can reflect on this healing experience. Feel proud of yourself for doing this. It is good and courageous! Bless you!

Chapter Nine : "The Father and I Are One"

Perhaps the most significant impact credited to technology over the last twenty years is the obvious need and ability to connect throughout our global society. Everywhere there is the constant increase of visible human circuitry through the continuous use of computers, cell phones, beepers, the World Wide Web, e-mail, voice mail, and broadband communication. We are perpetually reaching out to each other, person-to-person linking, information, creativity, economics, daily news, international weather, chat rooms, and horoscopes, all available to everyone, as quick as a double-click.

Global news can feel like local news as it is repeatedly flashed in front of you, even as you sip your morning coffee. Your TV setup resembles a broadcasting station, complete with satellite dish and a super-wand remote controller. You can be entertained 24/7 by watching movies, sports, cartoons, history, biographies, home improvement, home shopping, stock market updates, and of course the "Cooking Channel."

Day into night this noisy companion can make you feel connected, maybe even somewhat involved. However, as you leave your home to forge the day's events, the faces in your neighborhood or at work still may not seem to be any happier, healthier, or more satisfied. I recently decided to conduct my own "experiment" as I drove back to my office after running an errand. I decided to count the "happy faces" I could find on the sidewalks over a three or four block distance. Out of the twenty-eight people I noticed, two appeared smiley! The rest were walking with an expression that made them look like they were smelling something really bad.

Technology continues to push all limits into a wireless web of visual-audio information connections, while the heart-to-heart threads become more frayed. Crime, violence, suicide bombers, threats of biochemical warfare, nuclear warfare, terrorism, and new diseases build more walls of fear into daily interactions.

More sadly, woven into these routines, however, is that these negativities have become normal, and so is the cautious emotional detachment that goes with it. The secure person has invested in remote locks for cars, "the club" for steering wheels, home surveillance equipment, and a "nanny cam"— proof that safety has become a commodity rather than a natural result of a discerning trust in humanity.

Ironically we are designed to connect and to relate. We are coded to talk, listen, learn, explore, and to feel a sense of belonging to others. Abraham Maslow describes this belongingness as a primary need in all humans that assures individual development and security. Despite this basic need, calling out to be heard, technology doesn't seem to be truly listening to the real voice. Even with all the bells and whistles, the world does not feel closer, just more complicated by new fears. Certainly the terror that occurred in New York, Pennsylvania, and Washington, DC, on September 11, 2001 continues to echo with these new fears loud enough for all to hear, as we continue to live our lives as normally as possible. Day to day the memory remains now, recreating our routines with more technology in airports, schools, municipalities, border control, sports events, and public gatherings, with still no promise to children that their world will be any safer. Government officials and CNN TV runners periodically reinforce that we need to stay on the alert. Perhaps these signals are a blessing, causing an awareness that can sharpen our senses into a new resolve. Maybe the resolution is not to be found solely through radar and scanning devices.

Maybe the missing link is natural and safely placed inside everyone? I remember not wanting to move away from the TV for days on end after the shock of September 11, 2001. I wanted to know every detail, feel every emotion, because it all seemed so surreal. I watched the rescue and recovery through many sleepless nights. I listened to news reporters take their time and interview the family members who were so desperately looking for and hoping to find their loved ones. I watched and saw such rejoicing from TV personalities and crews when a survivor was found. Weeks and weeks went by with one heroic deed after another. Almost every day for weeks we heard "God Bless America" coming from somewhere. And, even though there was so much pain and tragedy, it felt good to drive to work and see flags on homes, cars, and lapels. People seemed to slow down a little, and kindness was obvious. I couldn't stop my tears every time I looked into a rescue worker's eyes as the nightly news kept its vigil at Ground Zero.

And then it occurred to me—the missing link! It is natural! It is in everyone! The firefighters, rescue workers, doctors, nurses, and the average bystander did not quickly read a book about courage and compassion before reaching out to help the stranger in need—they just DID IT. This is the most precious gift of such a disaster. It proved real courage and compassion are natural and will abundantly flow when each one just simply responds to the need. The wisdom and stamina that is called for is already within. This is the direct result of everyone's spiritual DNA. Each one is already and always will be connected to the Life Force of God the Father. And when that innate Power is triggered by pure intentionality to love and to help, real miracles just flow. If we could just keep this reality always in our hearts, then the thousands of lost lives have served us well.

A year has passed since that atrocity, and you have probably noticed humanity has slipped back a bit into its normal rushing again. American flags aren't so plentiful and road rage is gearing up again. So what happened? What is the truth about humankind? Is it normal to slack off? Is it natural to only "rise" to the occasion?

I believe if you don't know what is natural and always available, you're more likely to stay in the normal band of mediocracy, and without the deep understanding of your spiritual DNA and how to use it, you are more prone to feeling disconnected inside and more apt to look for Power outside. This search for Power outside leads the way for unhealthy competition, prejudice, power by title not effort, and fear of not knowing how to get the control.

Many of the ills of society are caused by this Power outside misconception, and again the resulting situations all seem too normal. Attempts to hide monies such as to not pay taxes, misuse of company "perks," insurance fraud, politicians and law enforcers who live "above the law," racketeering, illegal political favors, misuse of welfare and its benefits are all examples of a wounded psyche that doesn't know how to connect to the Power inside. It will then seek to find Power outside of self and try to store it, save it, manipulate it, always fearing someone else might take it.

No matter what, you are always having a relationship with Power. If it is perceived by you to be something outside of you, much of your energies and affects will be about getting it and keeping it, or brooding about not having it. The truth, however, is much simpler. You ARE a relationship with Power, Real Power, and that reality is God. From the Old Testament, Isaiah hears the Voice of God and knows His Power is eternal: "Behold, I am with you always." Another beautiful reference to the loving, protecting generosity of God in relationship to all people can be found in Psalm 23:

> The Lord is my shepherd, I shall not want;
>
> He makes me lie down in green pastures.
>
> He leads me beside still waters
>
> He restores my soul.
>
> He leads me in paths of righteousness for his name's sake.

Even though I walk through the valley of the shadow of death,

I fear no evil.

For thou art with me; thy rod and thy staff, they comfort me.

Thou preparest a table before me in the presence of my enemies;

Thou anointest my head with oil,

My cup overflows.

Surely goodness and mercy shall follow me all the days of my life;

And I shall dwell in the house of the Lord forever.

Every line brings poetry to the loving, steadfast Power of the Father Principle in its highest spiritual essence. The reliability of the relationship between God and humanity is clear and bold ("Thy rod and thy staff, they comfort me"). As I repeat these words, the Law of the Father Principle is written in my heart with great certainty!

In the New Testament, these themes are echoed by Jesus: "The Father and I are one." The Aramaic word ETH-PHATAH, which was used by Jesus, can be translated as "Be open to unity—reconnect with it."

Another powerful Aramaic is the word ABWOON. It has several translations, all indicating this same Divine Relationship, Our Father, Silent Potency, the Creative Process of each Moment.

From these root meanings, you can begin to understand how to use the Divine Relationship within you for all needs, trials, and celebrations. The word SHEM in Aramaic means "name." It also was used by Jesus to mean vibration, light. As you connect the ABWOON and SHEM together, you can grasp the true potency as Jesus stated, "Ask, and it will be given you; seek and you will find; knock and it will be opened to you" (Matt. 6:7-8).

Another example of the everlasting, ever-present Divine relationship and its promises is stated in Luke 18-27: "What is impossible with men is possible with God."

To help you make this Divine Relationship more tangible and practical, imagine that you have inherited this Power and its access through your spiritual gene pool—like a person whose biological father was an artist, who would be born with a propensity for this talent whether he or she knew it or not, or used it or not. The gift would be in your family name. You might think of yourself as Robert-God Powered, Maryann-God Powered.

This is not to imply that you are a self-inflated, ego-charged person. On the contrary, through acknowledging your ongoing relationship with God you will be able to really feel all aspects of your humanness, including the fears, struggles, joys, and delights. But as you continue through each day, you can now stay confident and stretch past any apparent limits.

The reference that comes to mind here is Moses when God commissioned him to be a leader and to be the father of His Laws. As Moses realized the destiny prepared by God, he questioned himself and God by asking, "Who am I that I should go to Pharaoh and bring the sons of Israel out of Egypt?" And the Lord said, "I will be with you; tell them the God of your fathers has sent you" (Exodus 3:11-14).

It is with this same authority from within that you can change, heal, create anything in your life. You might begin by visualizing that there is a spiritual identity in every cell of your being and that is made of light. This is the ABWOON (breath) of God permanently present. Practice sensing this Light in a childlike way by imagining that you swallowed sunshine! Then continue your day feeling that inner glow! Bring that glow to work, as you're driving, mowing the lawn, or doing the laundry. The more routinely you keep this in your mind and heart, the more you are releasing your naturally inherited Power! You will feel and stay inspired (in-Spirit!). Eventually, the Glowing Presence will be activated in everything you do, say, think, and feel. You will then come to the beautiful realization that within there breathes a Sacred Unity—a divine dance of you and God, Your Heavenly Father.

You can cultivate this Sacred Unity by watching nature. Witness how plants continue to grow and change with the season, all sourced by the invisible. Practice using affirmations daily. Write them on index cards to place at obvious sites—night stand, car visor, bathroom mirror, sock drawer. Repeat them to yourself: "I am sourced by the Divine Light within. All that I do, say, think, and feel is guided and directed by God's Divine right Action. I feel God's presence with me all day, every day."

The results are liberating and transforming. Let us prepare for a specific Prayer Room exercise.

Prayer Room Exercise: Are You Willing to Partner With God?

- Enter into your Prayer Room as outlined in Chapter One.
- Allow yourself to take a few deep breaths as you are surrounded by the Blue White Light entering in from the skylight above.
- Focus on that Light and really breathe it deeper and deeper into your

entire being.

- Take another deep breath and silently repeat to yourself, "Peace, Peace, Peace."

- Allow yourself to respond openly and honestly to the following questions:

  - re you really aware that the very breath you are breathing is the full Power and Presence of God?

  - Are you willing to shift your beliefs to trust in this inside Power, first, as the Life Force of the Universe? Are you ready to be in the world, but not of it?

  - What changes in yourself, your home, work, relationships have to happen in order to make this shift?

  - Are you willing to make these changes, even if they make you uncomfortable, or make your present life situations temporarily inconvenient?

  - If not, what is stopping you from making these changes in your values, attitudes, actions?

  - Do you understand that God always has a relationship with you?

  - Are you finally willing to make your partnership with God your primary relationship?

  - Do you understand that that is what is meant by "Seek first the kingdom and everything else shall follow" and the kingdom is within?

  - Do you realize that when you are in a true partnership with God, NOTHING IS IMPOSSIBLE?

– Are you ready to release the full potency of who you are?

• If so, repeat the following silently to yourself with conviction:

> I am always and forever connected to God, the Author of All Life. I am co-creator with God the Father Light and in this Divine Partnership I am able to do all things. I allow the Father Light to help me, heal me, guide me, and direct me into the highest good for all concerned. I am safe and loved in this Sacred Unity. Thank you. Amen, amen, amen.

• Relax and take your time and simply feel the Presence of God, loving you.

• Take your time and then ascend the Golden Steps out of your Prayer Room and back out into outer consciousness.

You may repeat this often. It increases your faith and confidence in both yourself and God.

Chapter Ten: The Gifts of Abba

As life was approaching the turn of the century into the second millennium, the term paradigm shift was often used. This was to imply a "change" or something different about how the world would function and how the "lay of the land" would advance. Of course, technology once again would be a major part of this shift. Ideas like one-world banking, balance of food and its distribution, ecological purification for water supplies, solar-power homes, wireless electronics, electronic automobiles, holistic health care, and pharmaceuticals to maintain youth and control or eliminate diseases were all targeted to be mainstreamed activities. Even though these ideas are not new, the projection appeared to be an idealism made available for everyone. Some would say that humanity was finally at a breaking-point realization that said, "We must find a better way."

I would suppose that every population at the turn of a millennium said something similar, only to have some decades pass with the human history of war, famine, and disease still repeating itself. Even the promise of new leadership, new government policies having made some in-roads can appear to be business as usual over time.

I do believe humanity has the answers. Perhaps more so now than ever, there can be an unprecedented union of technology and well-directed human spirit. I believe and trust that as everyone identifies, heals, and releases the true powers of the Father Principle, all will be enriched recipients of the "Gifts of Abba."

A clearer understanding of this ensues as the Hebrew meaning of Abba is reviewed. Abba in Hebrew means Daddy, Papa. It was used in the Old Testament when God was revealed to make a covenant with His people. Prior to this, the word Yahweh was used to identify God. Yahweh literally translated means, "I am that I am."

The connotation in the expression Yahweh was the All-Mighty, the Author of the Cosmos, and everything and everyone contained in it. It was a Power so awesome, it was almost fear. This is best demonstrated by the fact that the calling, saying, or mentioning of the word Yahweh was reserved for High Holy Days.

However, as God made His covenant with humanity, the same all-knowing, all-powerful God called Himself Abba to clearly define a much more endearing, close-at-hand, loving father, ready to help, protect, and direct His children. His covenant became a promise to all who call Him Abba, that they would be satisfied.

In Aramaic, the word for day, as it is used in the Lord's Prayer, "Give us thy daily bread," can mean any illuminated moment, not necessarily a twenty-four hour day. It also means a circle of needs according to the size of your family or the extent of your responsibility.

The Aramaic word for bread (lachma) can also mean understanding. It's not only physical food, but also nurturing for levels of our lives including mind, body, emotions, and spirit.

The Gifts of Abba are a promise, a covenant that whatever you are in need of can be fulfilled. Abba is the Spirit, the Breath within you. It is the Universal Intelligence that is ever-present in every breath.

The more you "go within" and become familiar with the feeling of this Presence, the more you can recognize all the gifts that await you. By repeated practical use of the Prayer Room, for example, you can become more "at home" in yourself, for yourself. You will then begin to feel the Presence of Abba, a truly Loving Father who has fashioned you in the palms of His own hands, and you will no longer feel separated from truth, wisdom, joy, love, healing. Instead, you will be quite confident that these gifts have been safely stored within you so that the way of the disjointed world would not steer you into an inner emptiness. Through the daily gifts of Abba, you can be in the world but not of it!

Some beautiful evening, look to the evening sky. Remain silent for five or ten minutes; look through darkness and observe the shimmering light in every star. Countless, wide and deep, every star is like the treasured gems of guidance, courage, determination, justice, and right action that are already inside you. The same Cosmos Almighty Father that created the sky softly breathes inside you as the Abba caring for you, a true child of God. Like that canopy sky, as above so below, on earth as it is in heaven, you can be in total connection with all these gifts, merely by asking in the silence of your heart.

The gifts of Abba are not only present in each individual; I believe events and/or situations, both positive and negative, can occur to prompt the individual to "go within." Sometimes in desperate hours or overwhelming joy a feeling, an epiphany, can be experienced that lets the person know there is more to me than just me. The unexplainable can also invite a deeper soul search to begin. Often these invitations to pray and rely on Abba as your partner happen through national and global experiences. Natural disasters, sudden tragedies, and great discoveries can all trigger this inward connection.

Most predominantly, great individuals who exemplify the Father Principle can have profound impact on the way humanity thinks, acts, feels. Gandhi, Martin Luther King, Jr., Mother Theresa, Albert Schweitzer, Albert Einstein, Mayor Rudolph Giuliani, Mohamad Ali, Eleanor Roosevelt, Nelson Mandela, Madame Curie, Susan B. Anthony, and Rosa Parks are just a few wonderful people whose lives illustrate the Father Principle at work.

Television and movies also can show a variety of expression that can trigger the Father Principle in its viewers. "The Bill Cosby Show," "NYPD Blue," "Boston Public," and "The District" illustrate some of the many faces of the day-to-day experiences involving an interaction with the aspects of the Father Principle.

"To Kill a Mockingbird," "Guess Who's Coming to Dinner?" "Yentl," "Field of Dreams," and of course "It's a Wonderful Life" all personify the Father Principle through the experiences of their main characters. A more recent example that perhaps illustrates the magnifying powers of the Father Principle is the movie "Pay It Forward." In this movie, the magnanimous effects of the Abba within are put into action through the commitment of an eleven-year-old boy! The message of this script is an urging for all, "We can make a difference!" Personally, I loved this movie, and I suggest it for parents and teachers as a way of planting Father Principle "seeds" in young people that will promise a better tomorrow!

Your gifts await you. Abba awaits you. There is nothing to do but to do it. The more you allow yourself to be connected from inside first, acknowledging this Power as the Source of ALL life, the more your LIFE will be sourced by ALL that you need. You will continuously, endlessly, abundantly be guided, directed, and protected by its Wisdom and Love.

Let us prepare for a particular Prayer Room exercise that is designed to "Give you your daily bread."

Prayer Room Exercise

- Allow yourself to enter into your Prayer Room as outlined in Chapter One.

- Allow yourself to take a few deep breaths and relax. Take your time.

- Allow the Blue White Light to continuously flow through you and around you throughout this prayerful exercise.

- Now silently repeat the following prayer to yourself.

> Abba, Abba, Oh Father of all that is Good and Holy in me, and around me!
>
> Bless me today! Bless me abundantly in Your Wisdom, Love, and Divine Right Action!
>
> Heal my soul of its weariness, comfort my body, calm my mind and open my heart to the richness of Gifts You have already given me.
>
> Release me, oh Holy One, from all thoughts, feelings, behaviors that do not serve my true Loving Self.
>
> Help me to forgive my offenders, forgive me if I have offended anyone, including myself, and give me the courage and strength to always follow what is good for me and the highest good of all.
>
> Direct me, today, oh Loving Father, so that I might hear You, feel You, and follow Your divine, loving, just ways.
>
> Do this, now and every day, so that in truth, I will feel my true worth and know it is You through me carrying me into daily

success, in Your Name.

Thank You, Heavenly Father, who forever lives in my heart.

Amen, amen, amen.

- When you are comfortable to do so, ascend the Golden Light stairs, back to outer consciousness, relaxed and refreshed.

In conclusion, may you use the practical advantage of your Prayer Room often and daily. May you come to know and feel your true worth, and may you see the world is a better place because of it!

— PEACE —

Bibliography

Allen, James. As a Man Thinketh. New York: Barnes & Noble, 1992.

Chopra, Deepak. The Seven Spiritual Laws. San Rafael, CA: Amber-Allen, 1994.

Curtis, Donald. How to Be Great. North Hollywood, CA: Wilshire, 1978.

Des Roches, Brian. Reclaiming Your Self. New York: Dell, 1990.

Dyer, Wayne. Manifest Your Destiny. New York: Harper Collins, 1997.

Grof, Stanislaw, M.D. Holotropic Mind. New York: Harper Collins, 1990.

Hay, Louise. You Can Heal Your Life. Santa Monica, CA: Hay House, 1984.

Holmes, Ernest. The Science of Mind. New York: Dodd, Mead and Co., 1938.

Kindlon, Dan, Ph.D., and Michael Thompson, Ph.D. Raising Cain. New York: Ballantine Books, 1999.

Nourven, Henri. Here and Now. New York: Crossroads, 1994.

Ruiz, Don Miguel. The Four Agreements. San Rafael, CA: Amber-Allen, 1997.

— — —. The Mastery of Love. San Rafael, CA: Amber-Allen, 1999.

Sagan, Carl. Broca's Brain. New York: Random House, 1974.

Silva, Jose. The Silva Mind Control Method. New York: Simon & Schuster, Inc., 1977.

Stevens, Anthony. Archetypes. London, England: Routledge & Kegan Ltd., 1982.

Stone, Robert, Ph.D. The Secret Life of Your Cells. West Chester, PA: 1989.

Walsch, Neale Donald. Conversations With God, Book I. New York: G. P. Putnam's Sons, 1995.